KNOW
YOUR
RIGHTS

KNOW YOUR RIGHTS

THE CONSUMER'S HANDBOOK

This edition produced 1992 for Betterware Limited by
Octopus Illustrated Publishing
Michelin House, 81 Fulham Road,
London SW3 6RB
part of Reed International Books Limited

Printed in Great Britain by Collins, Glasgow

CONTENTS

ONE

HELP AND ADVICE

How the Courts Can Help

If you have a complaint against a firm in regard to faulty goods or services and they refuse to take any steps to refund your money, repair the goods or do whatever else you wish by way of recompense (bearing in mind their only legal obligation is to refund money or pay damages), then your only other option is to take the matter to court and to seek redress there.

1 **Before** going to court always follow up any verbal complaint with a written one addressed, and sent recorded delivery, to the managing director of the company concerned. Only if the response to this is totally negative should you resort to legal means.

2 **Before** going to court always get a 'second opinion' as to the soundness of your case. Give the details to someone at the local Citizens Advice Bureau or Consumer Advice Centre and take along all correspondence relevant to the dispute.

3 If you wish to proceed there are special systems designed to deal with consumer claims under a certain amount and it may be possible for you to pursue a claim without incurring major expenses even if you lose.

England and Wales: Small claims at the county court (under £500)
Scotland: Small claims at the sheriff court (under £750)
Northern Ireland: Different system, see Chapter Two.

The English Small Claims System

This procedure in the county courts is designed to provide a simple form of 'do-it-yourself' justice for those who have a complaint involving a sum of £500 or less. Arbitration is informal and easy for a lay person to cope with. There are no hefty legal bills to pay if you lose the case.

Small Claims – Step by Step

Step one: Go along to your local county court. The court will tell you in which court you should issue the summons – either where the defendant lives or where the cause of the action took place. Then – with the help of the court staff if necessary – fill in a Particulars of Claim form which is designed to contain full details of the claim.

This costs anything from £7 to £37 depending on the amount of the claim.

Step two: If the defendant decides not to dispute the claim, you can apply to the court for judgement in your favour to the effect that he must pay you. If the firm disputes your claim, then the case will automatically be heard under the informal arbitration procedures, except in special circumstances (if a very complex question of law is involved, for instance). A date for the preliminary hearing will be set.

Step three: You go along to the court for a five-minute appointment with the other party and the Registrar (the preliminary hearing). If the other party doesn't turn up you may get judgement in your favour if you can satisfy the Registrar that you have a case. Otherwise if everyone is there, the Registrar will order both sides to exchange lists of documents. He or she will also find out how many witnesses are to be called and so decide how long the case is likely to take. In a simple case s/he may make a decision there and then.

Step four: You go along to the court and attend the arbitration procedure – this is carried out by the Registrar, and the firm you are suing or their representative will also be present. The Registrar who hears the case can adopt any procedure he chooses – the intention being to allow both sides an equal opportunity to present their side of the dispute. The Registrar may even, should he so choose, go to take a look at defective workmanship for himself. No formal court proceedings are involved – it will be a question of sitting round a table and talking, without a wig or gown in sight!

You can call witnesses, but in the case of an expert's testimony it is normally best to present this in the form of a written report.

Step five: The Registrar will come to a decision on the basis of the evidence presented to him. That decision will be final and binding on both parties.

What Does it Cost?

If you win the case, the Registrar may order that you be paid the cost of taking out the summons. And if you used the independent evidence of an expert witness – e.g. you had upholstery fabric tested to show it was not of an acceptable standard – you could get the cost of this paid to you.

If you lose you do not suffer the heavy legal costs you might expect to in an ordinary trial, which is why this small claims procedure is so important for the consumer.

Even if the opposing side brings along a solicitor to act on their behalf, and you lose, you will not have to bear the other side's costs as under this system neither side is able to recover solicitors' costs. You will, of course, have had the initial cost of taking out the summons but this is not so large as to be prohibitive.

Do You Need a Solicitor?

This is very much a 'do-it-yourself' type of justice, established as such over a number of years, and county courts are quite accustomed to people conducting their own cases. The procedure is simple, the atmosphere very relaxed and the Registrar generally helpful.

But it is important to marshal all the relevant facts before going to court and to take copies of all receipts, correspondence and documents. Also be precise about dates. Even the most helpful registrar is likely to become irritated if someone is constantly shuffling around trying to find the correct papers.

■ Take a friend along for moral support.

■ Get a copy of *Small Claims and the County Court* from county courts or Citizens Advice Bureaux.

The Scottish Small Claims System

A new small claims procedure in the sheriff court was introduced at the end of 1988.

All claims for £750 and below are heard as small claims and where there is an alternative claim to money up to the £750 limit, people can use the procedure to force a provider of services to fulfil their legal obligations. For instance, a tenant could force a landlord to undertake minor repairs.

Expenses are not awarded for claims under £200. For claims between £200 and £750, the maximum expenses that may be awarded are £75.

You are allowed to take someone who is not a solicitor to represent you if you wish. If you choose to use a solicitor, the expenses limit may make the case rather expensive.

If there is a hearing, like the English system, it will be informal and the usual technical legal rules about how to present a case don't apply.

Forms and explanatory leaflets and guidebooks are available from local sheriff courts and Citizens Advice Bureaux. Trading Standards Departments can also give advice.

Northern Ireland

Here one can go to the county court where there is a small claims arbitration system to deal with amounts of under £500. There is, as in the English and Welsh small claims system, an initial fee to get things going. Normally, even if you lose your case, there will be no other costs involved in taking legal action.

For further details of the system get a copy of *Small Claims – The New Procedure in Northern Ireland*, which is available free from most Citizens Advice Bureaux.

Claims for Larger Amounts

Even if one's claim is for more than £500 (or £750 in Scotland, £500 in Northern Ireland), it can still be pursued through the courts – but it may cost more than legal action under the special small claims systems.

In England and Wales one would take action through the county court. It could still be conducted on an arbitration basis – but **only** if both parties agree to this, can the Registrar decide to deal with it this way. Otherwise, the procedure will be that of any formal court and if you lose, you will be liable for the other party's costs.

In Scotland a claim for over £750 comes under the heading of an 'ordinary cause' and the case is heard in the sheriff court.

In Northern Ireland claims over £500 are dealt with by the county court, but here again it may be expensive.

While you could conduct your own case for these larger claims, it is generally advisable to consult a solicitor initially.

If You Need an Expert Witness or an Independent Report

■ Ask the advice of the local Consumer Advice Centre if there is one in your area. They may be able to provide a list of local firms who will undertake independent inspection and test work.

■ Check with a nearby college of domestic science. They sometimes carry out tests on household goods, fabrics and so on.

■ For cars, the *Institute of Automotive Engineer Assessors*, 1 Love Lane, London EC2V 1JJ, will provide a list of local members who do technical examinations and may act as arbitrators in disputes. **Charges vary.**

■ An independent laboratory will carry out investigations and provide reports for consumer complaints on a variety of goods from garments to carpets. Methods of testing are those recommended by the British Standards Institution's International Standards Organization and other official bodies. They charge a fee which varies according to the work.

■ Citizens Advice Bureaux, Consumer Advice Centres or Trading Standards Departments will have details of testing houses.

TWO

WHERE TO GO FOR HELP/ INFORMATION/ ADVICE

The following information and addresses should prove useful when looking for help, information or advice on consumer matters.

Citizens Advice Bureau

This is a voluntary organization started in the thirties which has increased in importance ever since. There is a network of over 1,000 local bureaux in towns both large and small throughout the UK and the addresses are to be found in the local telephone directory or local library. The staff are all well trained and can give confidential and impartial advice on almost any problem from housing and legal difficulties to how to deal with faulty goods. Some bureaux have panels of solicitors, accountants, surveyors or other professionals who give free advice.

The bureaux can also provide leaflets on all sorts of subjects and can refer the public to other organi-

zations who give help in specialized fields. **Contact:**

The National Association of Citizens Advice Bureaux
Myddelton House
115-123 Pentonville Road
London N1 9LZ
(Tel: 01-833 2181)

or in Scotland

Scottish Association of Citizens Advice Bureaux
82 Nicolson Street
Edinburgh EH8 9EW
(Tel: 031-667 0156/7)
ADVICE FREE

Consumer Advice Centres

A pilot scheme was started in London in the seventies and ever since then centres have been set up in various towns throughout Britain (usually in or near main shopping centres for easy access). They are staffed and run by the local authority's Trading Standards or Consumer Protection Department. They can provide all kinds of consumer information and leaflets and take up complaints on one's behalf.

These centres can also provide extremely valuable advice before you buy something. They can, in that regard, provide information about the relative merits, performance, price and so on of products and this may well prevent problems at a later date and ensure that your purchase is the best value in your price range and suitable for your needs.

You can find out whether there is such a centre in your area by contacting the local authority. **ADVICE FREE**

Trading Standards/Consumer Protection Department

This is the department whose function it is to administer the legislation involving criminal offences in the consumer field, e.g. Trade Descriptions Act, Weights and Measures Act. Any contravention of laws or regulations should be reported to this department.

Trading Standards officers will also deal with a variety of problems connected with goods, selling methods, credit, short weight, holidays, motor vehicles and repairs, labelling, descriptions, bad service, broken contracts and so on. **Contact:**

In England, your local **Town Hall** for details of these departments or in Scotland, your local **Regional Authority** or in Northern Ireland, **Department of Commerce** 176 Newtonbreda Road Belfast BT8 4QS. **ADVICE FREE**

Environmental Health Department

This comes under the umbrella of local government and the officers in the department are there to enforce certain standards and also the law in regard to health, hygiene, food, home improvement, pollution, etc. They are concerned not only with standards and with legislation but will also be happy to give advice to the public on all such matters. If you find some dirty habit being practised in a shop this is the department to deal with it; similarly, if you get a rusty nail in your loaf of bread, or your local supermarket is selling goods which are bad. They enforce laws such as the Food Act and are much concerned with public health matters. **Contact:**

In Scotland, the offices of your **District Council.** In England and elsewhere, your local **Town Hall.** **ADVICE FREE**

Consumers' Association Personal Service

This non-profit-making organization, which produces *Which?* magazine and a number of extra supplements, also runs a personal advice service for a small annual fee. The association will deal with individual complaints and give detailed help and advice, often taking up the matter on behalf of the consumer. **Contact:**

Consumers' Association Dept BJJ 14 Buckingham Street London WC2N 6DS **ADVICE FOR A SMALL ANNUAL FEE**

The Media

There are television programmes on all channels and on local networks which deal with consumer problems at a very practical level, in the sense that the programme takes up the difficulty on behalf of the person concerned. There are radio programmes both at national and regional levels which do the same thing and many newspapers and magazines offer a similar service. All these media forms are effective in solving problems – but they do get so many sent in that it may only be possible for them to deal with a small percentage of those actually received. **ADVICE FREE**

The Police

Your local police force will have a crime prevention department and officers here will be prepared to offer advice and help to the public on such matters as keeping both your home, your car and any other property safe and secure. Someone will usually call round to your home if required.

They are very much concerned with road safety, vandalism and so on and officers give talks to schools, organizations and clubs on such themes. The Home Office issued a booklet, *Police and Public* – ask for this at your local station and try to get the National Consumer Council's booklet on how the police can offer advice and assistance to the public. **Contact:**

The Duty Officer at your police station who will refer you to an officer who specializes in the advice you're seeking.
ADVICE FREE

Libraries

Libraries have a whole range of free leaflets and staff can tell customers what reading material is available on particular subjects in regard to consumer rights. Libraries should be able to provide addresses of local advice and legal centres.

Prestel

This is basically a television set connected by telephone to a computer and by pressing a button viewers who have their set suitably adapted can get 'pages' of information on all kinds of consumer matters. It is hoped that these sets will eventually be set up in public places where members of the public seeking help or information with consumer matters will have access.

The kind of advice and information available includes: rights and complaints in regard to advertising, mail order, repairs, services, car buying, holidays and other such matters.

Details of organizations giving advice are also available 'on screen'. A private subscriber to the service pays for it with his telephone bill.

Self-Help (Consumer Groups)

Local consumer groups throughout Britain – some 50 of them – are linked to a central body. They are independent, voluntary organizations and members carry out surveys on everything from shoe shops to gas prices, producing written reports of their work which are sent to the organizations concerned. By such techniques, groups have achieved considerable success. **Contact:**

National Federation of Consumer Groups
12 Mosley Street
Newcastle-upon-Tyne
NE1 1DE.

Solicitors

There are various sources of free legal advice, for instance, law centres or legal advice centres. Some of these are run by local university law departments on a voluntary basis, others by groups of solicitors. To find your nearest law centre contact:

Legal Action Group
242 Pentonville Road
London N1 9UN.

Your local Citizens Advice Bureau will almost certainly be able to provide a legal advice service by a qualified solicitor at certain times of the week. It will be free.

Any solicitor will give advice on a fee basis. Many, but not all, offer a 'fixed fee interview' which simply means that for up to half an hour of their time they will charge only £5.

NOTE: It is important, if you want to take advantage of this scheme, that you make it quite clear from the beginning – or you might find yourself being charged a lot more!

This fixed fee interview does not apply in Northern Ireland. Apart from this special scheme, solicitors' fees vary from one part of the country to another and can also depend on the type of work, the seniority of the person doing it and payments which must be made in connection with the case. As a rough guide, charges could be between £20 to £60 an hour.

So always ask first what the charges are likely to be.

For those with limited financial resources there is a legal advice and assistance scheme, more commonly known as the Green Form Scheme. It is based on a means test and intended to give cheap (or comple-tely free) legal assistance for preliminary work, and not necessarily to cover complete costs. In Scotland the Pink Form Scheme is similar.

Legal Aid, on the other hand, can pay **all** costs if a case goes to court. Whether or not you qualify for this also depends on income level and sometimes the type of case (it's not available for industrial tribunals, for instance).

For more details on such aid, get leaflets from Citizens Advice Bureaux or Consumer Advice Centres – they are called *Legal Aid – Financial Limits* and *Legal Aid Guide*.

To find a solicitor, consult the Yellow Pages under 'Solicitor' or check the Law Society's Directory of Services in your local library.

Consumer Organizations

**Agricultural Consumers'
Committee for Great Britain and
Committee for England and Wales**
Room 642
Great Westminster House
Horseferry Road
London SW1P 2AE

or

Consumers' Committee Scotland
Chesser House
Gorgie Road
Edinburgh EH11

The Great Britain committee will deal with complaints about potatoes for the whole of Britain. The England and Wales and the Scotland Committees deal with complaints about milk. Complaints should be sent to the appropriate address.

British Standards Institution
Park Street
London W1A 2BS.

It sets standards for goods and the goods which are of a certain standard in terms of passing the BS tests bear a label known as the Kitemark (see page 69). The Institution also has a number of booklets – list on application.

British Standards Institution's Quality Assurance Department
Maylands Avenue
Hemel Hempstead
Herts.

They will deal with complaints about products carrying the BS Kitemark.

Consumers' Association
14 Buckingham Street
London WC2N 6DS.

The organization was founded in 1957 and funded purely by subscriptions from members. It publishes *Which?* magazine and a wide variety of books on consumer subjects. It runs a personal complaints service for an annual fee.

Design Council
The Design Centre
28 Haymarket
London SW1Y 4SU
or
72 Vincent Street
Glasgow G2 5TN.

The Design Council promotes well-designed products which also conform to safety standards. Goods are on show at the two centres and an index gives details of goods designed to serve their purpose. The centres handle public enquiries.

British Apparel Centre
7 Swallow Place
London W1R 7AA.

This is the recognized authority on care labelling on clothes.

Insurance Ombudsman Bureau
31 Southampton Row
London WC1B 5HJ.

This independent organization was set up in 1981. It will deal with complaints against insurance companies which subscribe to the Bureau.

Personal Insurance Arbitration Service
Chartered Institute of Arbitrators
75 Cannon Street
London EC4N 5BH.

National Consumer Council
20 Grosvenor Gardens
London SW1W 0DH.

or

Scottish Consumer Council
4 Somerset Place
Glasgow G3 7JT

or

Welsh Consumer Council
Oxford House
Hills Street
Cardiff CF1 2DR

or

General Consumer Council for Northern Ireland
176 Newtonbreda Road
Belfast BT8 4QS.

This was set up in 1975 by the Government to present the consumer's case to the Government. It speaks for consumers, carries out its own research and surveys and publishes the results. It also campaigns for consumers on all aspects of everyday life from shopping to transport and publishes a number of useful booklets, a list of which is available on request. It does not deal directly with complaints by the public.

National Federation of Consumer Groups
12 Mosley Street
Newcastle-upon-Tyne
NE1 1DE.

This is an organization with voluntary groups throughout the UK. Groups meet, carry out surveys, publish results and put pressure on the Government through the main organization.

Office of Fair Trading
15-25 Breams Buildings
Field House
London EC4A 1PR.

This was set up in 1973. It does not deal with individual complaints but collates data from consumer organizations. It is responsible for enforcing legislation such as the Consumer Credit Act.

Packaging Council
161-166 Fleet Street
London EC4.

This council will deal with complaints against packaging which haven't been satisfactorily explained by the individual packager.

Registrar of Friendly Societies and Offices of the Industrial Assurance Commissioner
17 North Audley Street
London W1Y 2AP

or

58 Frederick Street
Edinburgh EH2 1NB

or

Northern Ireland Registrar
43-47 Chichester Street
Belfast BT1 4RJ.

This organization deals with complaints about friendly societies, building societies and will arbitrate in any disputes concerning doorstep life insurance, trustee savings banks, National Savings Banks and some other types of national savings.

Where to Complain about Public Services

AIR
Air Transport Users' Committee
129 Kingsway
London WC2B 6NN
Complaints about airport facilities should go to the Airport Consultative Committee for the appropriate airport.

BUSES
Local Traffic Commissioner
(Address from your local authority)

COMPANIES
Companies House
Cardiff
CF4 3UZ.

COAL
Domestic Coal Consumers' Council
Gavrelle House
2 Bunhill Row
London EC1Y 8LL
This council will deal with complaints about sale and supply.

ELECTRICITY
The Electricity Consultative Council will deal with complaints against local electricity boards. (Address in showrooms or phone directory.)

GAS
Regional Gas Consumer Councils
(Addresses throughout the UK from the telephone directory, from your gas bill or showroom.)

OFGAS (Office of Gas Supply)
Southside
105 Victoria Street
London SW1E 6QT.

THE UNDERGROUND
The ticket office of the local underground service will usually display the address where you may write if you have a complaint.

POST
Post Office Users' National Council
Waterloo Bridge House
Waterloo Road
London SE1 8UA
(There are separate offices in Scotland, Wales and Northern Ireland – see phone book for details.)

Some Head Post Offices in towns throughout Britain have set up a Customer Relations Unit. Anyone with a complaint against postal services can phone the number given in the directory and the complaint will be dealt with. Edinburgh was one of the first to set this up and it is now to be found in various UK towns and cities.

TELEPHONES
Telecommunications Advice Committee (TAC) or **Advisory Committee on Telecommunications**
(Address in the phone book.)
also
OFTEL (Office of Telecommunications)
Atlantic House
Holborn Viaduct
London EC1N 2HQ.

RAIL
Transport Users' Consultative Committees
(There are 11 regional committees. Addresses from nearest railway station or telephone directory.)

Trade Associations

These look after their own members, but they will also deal with consumer complaints in some cases. Many have their own code of practice and their own conciliation or arbitration scheme to deal with consumer complaints.

ADVERTISING
Advertising Standards Authority
Brook House
2-16 Torrington Place
London WC1E 7HN

ANTIQUES
London and Provincial Antique Dealers' Association
3 Cheval Place
London SW7 1EW

BANKS
Office of Banking Ombudsman
Citadel House
5-11 Fetter Lane
London EC4A 1BR

BEDS
National Bedding Federation
251 Brompton Road
London SW3 2EZ

BUILDING AND
DECORATING
National House Building Council
58 Portland Place
London W1N 4BU
and
5 Manor Place
Edinburgh EH3 7DH
or
National Register of Warranted Builders
33 John Street
London WC1N 2BB
or
British Decorators' Association
6 Haywra Street
Harrogate
North Yorkshire

BUILDING SOCIETIES
The Office of the Building Societies Ombudsman
Grosvenor Gardens House
35-37 Grosvenor Gardens
London SW1X 7AW

CARAVANS
National Caravan Council
43-45 High Street
Weybridge, Surrey

CARPETS
The British Carpet Manufacturers' Association
Royalty House
72 Dean Street
London W1V 5HB
or
Carpet Cleaners' Association
Ventnor House
97 Knighton Field Road West
Leicester LE2 6LH

CARS
Motor Agents' Association
201 Great Portland Street
London W1N 6AB
or
Scottish Motor Trade Association
3 Palmerston Place
Edinburgh EH12 5AQ
or
Society of Motor Manufacturers and Traders
Forbes House
Halkin Street
London SW1X 7DS
or
Vehicle Builders' and Repairers' Association
Belmont House
Finkle Lane
Gildersome LS27 7TW

DIRECT MAIL AND TELEPHONE MARKETING
The British Direct Marketing Association
1 New Oxford Street
London WC1A 1NQ

DOOR-TO-DOOR SELLING AND PARTY PLAN SELLING
Direct Selling Association
44 Russell Square
London WC1B 4JP

DOUBLE GLAZING
Glass and Glazing Federation
44-48 Borough High Street
London SE1 1XB

ELECTRICAL GOODS
Radio, Electrical and Television Retailers' Association (RETRA)
Retra House
57-61 Newington Causeway
London SE1 6BE
or
Association of Manufacturers of Domestic Electrical Appliances (AMDEA)
Leicester House
8 Leicester Street
London WC2H YBN

ELECTRICAL WORK
Electrical Contractors' Association
ESCA House
34 Palace Court
London W2 4JG
or
Electrical Contractors' Association of Scotland
23 Heriot Row
Edinburgh EH3 6EW

ESTATE AGENTS
National Homes Network
Suite 501, Radnor House
93 Regent Street
London W1
or
National Association of Estate Agents
Arbon House
21 Jury Street

FINANCIAL SERVICES
Securities and Investment Board (SIB)
3 Royal Exchange Buildings
London EC3V 3NL
or
Association of Futures Brokers and Dealers (AFBD)
B Section, 5th Floor
Plantation House
4-16 Mincing Lane
London EC3M 3DX
or
Financial Intermediaries, Managers and Brokers Regulatory Association (FIMBRA)
Hertsmere House, Marsh Wall
London E14 9RQ
or
The Investment Management Regulatory Organisation (IMRO)
Centre Point
103 New Oxford Street
London WC1
or
The Life Assurance and Unit Trust Regulatory Organisation (LAUTRO)
Centre Point
103 New Oxford Street
London WC1
or
The Securities Association (TSA)
The Stock Exchange
London EC2N 1EQ

FOOD
Food Manufacturers' Federation
6 Catherine Street
London WC2B 5JJ

FURNITURE
National Association of Retail Furnishers
17-21 George Street
Croydon CR9 1TQ

or
The Scottish House Furnishers' Association
203 Pitt Street
Glasgow G2 4DB

FURNITURE REMOVERS
The British Association of Removers
279 Gray's Inn Road
London WC1X 8SY

GAS
Confederation for the Registration of Gas Installers (CORGI)
St Martin's House
140 Tottenham Court Road
London W1

HAIRDRESSING
Hairdressing Council
17 Spring Street
London W2

HEARING AIDS
Hearing Aid Council
40a Ludgate Hill
London EC4M 7DE

HEATING
Heating and Ventilating Contractors' Association
ESCA House
34 Palace Court
London W2 4JG

INSURANCE
Association of British Insurers
Aldermary House
10-15 Queen Street
London EC4
or
British Insurance and Investment Brokers Association
BIIBA House
14 Bevis Marks
London EC3A 7NT
or
The Manager – Customer Enquiries

Lloyds
London House
6 London Street
London EC3R 7AB

JEWELLERY
Jewellery Advisory Centre
30 St George Street
London W1R 9FA
or
National Association of Goldsmiths
St Dunstan's House
Carey Lane
London EC2V 8AB

LAUNDRY AND CLEANING
Textile Services Association
7 Churchill Court
58 Station Road
North Harrow HA2 7SA.

MAIL ORDER
**The Mail Order Traders'
Association of Great Britain**
25 Castle Street
Liverpool L2 7RA
or
Mail Order Publishers' Authority
1 New Burlington Street
London W1X 1FD
or
Mailing Preference Service
Freepost 22
London W1E 7EZ

PHOTOGRAPHY
**Association of Photographic
Laboratories**
9 Warwick Court
Gray's Inn
London WC1R 5DJ
or
**National Pharmaceutical
Association**
Mallinson House
40-42 St Peter's Street
St Albans AL1 3NT

PLUMBING
**National Association of Plumbing,
Heating and Mechanical Services
Contractors**
6 Gate Street
London WC2A 3HX
or
**Scottish and Northern Ireland
Plumbing Employers' Federation**
2 Walker Street
Edinburgh ED3 7LB
or
Institute of Plumbing
Scottish Mutual House
North Street
Hornchurch
Essex

SHOES
**British Footwear Manufacturers'
Federation**
Royalty House
72 Dean Street
London W1V 5HB
or
Footwear Distributors' Federation
Commonwealth House
1-19 New Oxford Street
London WC1A 1PA

SHOE REPAIRS
**National Association of Shoe
Repair Factories**
60 Wickham Hill
Hurstpierpoint
Hassocks
Sussex
or
**St Crispin's Boot Trades
Association**
St Crispin's House
21 Station Road
Desborough N16 2SA

SPECTACLES
**British College of Ophthalmic
Opticians (Optometrists)**
10 Knaresborough Place
London SW5 0TG

TOYS
**British Toy Manufacturers'
Association**
80 Camberwell Road
London SE5 0EG

TIMESHARE
Timeshare Developers Association
23 Buckingham Gate
London SW1E 6LB

TRAVEL
**Association of British Travel
Agents**
55-57 Newman Street
London W1P 4AH

Other Useful Addresses

ARBITRATION
Chartered Institute of Arbitrators
75 Cannon Street
London EC4N 5BH

ARCHITECTS AND
SURVEYORS
**Royal Institute of British
Architects**
66 Portland Place
London W1N 4AD
or
**Royal Institution of Chartered
Surveyors**
12 Great George Street
London SW1P 3AD
or
Scottish Branch RICS
7 Manor Place
Edinburgh EH3 7DN

BUSINESS REGISTRATION
The Registrar
LCCI Business Registry
London Chamber of Commerce
and Industry

69-73 Cannon Street
London EC4N 5AB

EQUAL OPPORTUNITIES
Equal Opportunities Commission
Overseas House
Quay Street
Manchester M3 3HN
or
Caerwys House
Windsor Place
Cardiff CF1 1LB
or
249 West George Street
Glasgow GS 4QE

LAW
The Law Society
113 Chancery Lane
London WC2A 1PL
or
The Law Society of Scotland
Law Societies Hall
P.O. Box 75
26 Drumshaugh Gardens
Edinburgh EH3 7YR
or
**The Incorporated Law Society of
Northern Ireland**
Royal Courts of Justice (Ulster)
Belfast B77 3JZ

MEDIA
BBC Television Centre
Wood Lane
London W12 8QT
or
**Independent Broadcasting
Authority**
70 Brompton Road
London SW3 1EY
or
Press Council
1 Salisbury Square
London EC4Y 8AE

THREE

BUYING

Shops

We have come a long way since the days of medieval markets when those offering goods for sale had few obligations to their customers and little responsibility for the quality of their wares. The onus was very much on the buyer to examine the merchandise, to check carefully for defects and to rely entirely on his own judgement before handing over his money.

Today the whole concept of shopping has changed. There is a quite bewildering choice of both goods and materials on offer. Many products are prepacked, with bubbles of plastic or boxes of cardboard which leave little opportunity for the customer to examine them for quality and quantity.

We are all, nevertheless, concerned with getting value for money and so, over the years, consumer organisations and others have spent a great deal of time encouraging and persuading both manufacturers and retailers to give us more information. There are labelling regulations covering such things as content and weight – voluntary schemes to indicate quality, performance or design and to tell us how to look after a particular product to get the best use from it. There are laws to ensure that descriptions and information given to the consumer are accurate. The wise shopper is the one who makes use of all the available information before buying.

Labels to Look Out For

There are some 'general advice' labels which are to be found on a wide variety of products. They will indicate the standard of performance one might expect from the article, or that it has passed certain strict tests, or perhaps that it is considered to be particularly well designed. Examples of these are:

■ The **Kitemark** seen only on articles which have passed stringent tests and have been made in accordance with the relevant British Standard. There are standards covering all kinds of products from motor-cycle helmets to school blazers and carpets. There are over 8,000 British Standards and 400 of them are for consumer goods.

■ The **British Standards Safety Mark** to be found on things like cookers, fires, boilers and light fittings and is an indication that they comply with safety standards.

■ The **Design Council Label** appearing on British goods which have been selected as being well made, well designed and practical to use. An index of all such goods is available in the London and Glasgow Design Centres.

■ The **British Gas Seal of Service** guaranteeing parts and labour of an appliance bought and installed by British Gas for one year and indicating the availability of spare parts for a certain period. It also assures the customer that installation is carried out to certain standards.

Food Labelling

With some foods it's easy to tell at a glance what you are getting. An orange for instance is easily recognisable as such and so is a potato. But today meat may well have a soya content which is not immediately obvious to the shopper looking at it displayed in the chill cabinet and when a product is encased in tin or wrapped in cardboard, then the only clue the shopper has to its contents is the label on the outside. This is why it is so important that we be given a certain amount of information on these labels: the Food Act and the Food Labelling Regulations make sure that we do get that information. The main facts on a label are:

■ the name or description of the food
■ what it's made from
■ how long you can keep it and under what conditions
■ its weight, volume or number in the pack
■ perhaps its place of origin
■ preparation or cooking instructions where necessary
■ the name and address of the manufacturer, packer or seller.

The actual name of the food must be given on the label or packet – in addition to any brand name. A tin of ham could not, for instance, simply have the words 'John South's' on the label – it has to be actually named as 'ham'. And, on fresh food labelling, the particular variety must also be given. So for potatoes, the pack should indicate whether the variety is 'Desiree', 'Pentland Crown' or whatever.

The illustrations on labels which are designed to indicate the nature of the contents must not be too far-fetched or downright misleading. Certain foods must not be described in terms which might well give the shopper a wrong impression. Liqueur chocolates, for instance, must actually contain a significant quantity of liqueur – if they don't then the label must describe them as being merely 'liqueur flavoured'.

Food sold not in packets or tins but simply displayed on the counter or shelf should have some sort of ticket prominently placed nearby and this should have written on it the name or description of the particular food, and the category names of any additives it contains, e.g. 'Black Pudding. Contains colour and preservatives'.

Date Marking
Most food (exceptions below) must be date marked to indicate its minimum durability using the words 'best before' followed by the day, month and year. The exceptions are:

- Perishable food (with a life of up to six weeks) instead of 'best before' may use the words 'sell by' followed by the day and month only, plus an indication of how long after purchase the food will keep, if properly stored.
- Food with a life of up to three months may omit the year.
- Food lasting between three months and 12 months may omit the day and use 'best before end' followed by the month and the year.

The date mark on foods (of whichever durability) should be accompanied by instructions for storing the product, so that it will remain in good condition until the specified date, e.g. 'keep refrigerated'.

Some foodstuffs, however, don't have to carry a date mark – they are: fresh fruit and vegetables; some bread and pastries; vinegar; cooking salt; sugar; chewing gum; cheese which is specifically intended to reach maturity while in its packaging; most alcoholic drinks, except beer; food that lasts for more than 18 months, for example some canned goods.

Additives
The ingredients list must also show any additives that have been used as ingredients in foods. Most approved additives have an identifying number. The numbering system was introduced as a simple code to avoid putting long chemical names on labels. If the additive has been approved by the European Community, as well as by the UK, there is an 'E' in front of the number. An additive may be shown in the ingredients list either by its number or by its proper name or both. Usually a category name, such as 'preservative', must come before the additive to tell you its purpose.

25

Flavourings are not yet controlled in this way, although they may only be used in food if they are safe. The label must state that flavourings have been used but need not list them by name.

What do the Words on the Food Labels Mean?

- **Antioxidant** To stop fat becoming rancid
- **Autolysed yeast** A yeast extract flavouring
- **Caramel** A colouring – found even in brown vinegar
- **Citric acid** A natural fruit acid for flavouring
- **Edible gum** A thickening substance
- **Emulsifier** Combines oil and water to give a good texture and stop ingredients separating out once blended
- **Hydrolized vegetable protein** Enhances flavour
- **Lactose** A milk sugar which is used for flavouring
- **Monosodium glutamate** Enhances the flavour of the product
- **Permitted colouring** Any one of the many artificial or natural colourings which can be added to food (not all colours can be)
- **Preservative** Normally sorbic acid – prevents harmful organisms forming, retards spoilage
- **Saccharin** An artificial sweetener
- **Starch/modified starch** Thickens the product and is usually made mainly from maize
- **Tricalcium phosphate** Prevents foodstuffs from forming lumps

Nutrition Labelling

Information about nutrition – for example, how much energy a food provides, or how much fat it contains – is not required by law. But many manufacturers and retailers are now providing this. In the future, a standardised presentation is likely to be required by law.

At present Government guidelines suggest a standard format to prevent confusion. To help you compare products easily, labels show how much of a nutrient there is in 100 grams (about three and a half ounces) of the food. This also gives an indication of the proportion of the nutrients in a helping.

According to the manufacturer's resources or the size of the label, the amount of nutrition information is either simple – protein, carbohydrate and fat together with the total energy provided – or more detailed.

Extra detail will give a breakdown of the different types of carbohydrate and fat, together with information about sodium and fibre. This extra detail is important for people following special diets who need to identify, for example, the amount of saturates or saturated fatty acids, which are generally thought to be one of the causes of heart and other cardiovascular diseases.

Claims for Particular Benefits

There are restrictions on claims made about food. Our laws contain general rules to prevent misleading claims and descriptions but for some claims there are more specific controls. These cover claims that food is suitable for particular people such as diabetics or slimmers, for example:

- 'high in polyunsaturates' or 'low in cholesterol'
- 'contains vitamins and minerals'
- cures illness or disease.

Eggs

EEC regulations cover the labelling of eggs and require that certain information be given on the pack:

- The name and address of the packer
- The number of eggs packed
- The number of the packing station
- The number of the week in which it was packed. The week number goes from 1 to 52 with week 1 as the week which includes 1 January every year.

On the outside of most individual egg boxes there will be a self-adhesive label showing part of the required information in the form of a code, although sometimes this is stamped straight on to the box, rather than the label. That code can be deciphered as follows:

- The first number indicates in which country the eggs were packed. The UK number is 9.
- The second number tells you which UK area the eggs come from.
- The last number is that of the actual packing station in which the eggs were packed.

So from the numbers shown on the label, you could work out that the eggs were packed in the twenty-third week of the year, in Britain (more particularly in the East Midlands) and the packing station in that area was number 890. If you wished to decode the area number, you could contact the local office of the Ministry of Agriculture, Fisheries and Food (under 'Agriculture' in the phone book). The size is not regarded as part of the code, although it is marked.

These labelling regulations apply mainly to eggs which are sold in shops. If eggs are sold at the farm gate, in a local market or even door-to-door they need not comply with the EEC regulations.

Vegetables

Under EEC regulations vegetables are subject to a system of grading and the grading must be displayed with the produce. There are four classes of quality:

- **Class 1** indicates that the vegetables are of the very best quality with no defects
- **Class 2** is still of good quality but there may be some minor defects, such as a blemish
- **Class 3** describes products of a lower standard

There is also what's known as an 'extra class' used only to describe produce of supreme quality, perhaps limited in availability. The grading information given alongside vegetables will normally be reflected in different prices being charged for the various classes.

Wine

EEC regulations require that the following appear on the label on the bottle:
- Type of wine. If 'quality' wine, the region of origin
- The country of origin
- The name and address of the importer/bottler
- Wine bottled after August 1977 must have a statement giving the nominal volume of the contents based on an average assessment.

Under the laws of *appellation controlée* relating to French wine, if an *appellation controlée* wine displays the name of a particular vineyard or chateau it must have actually been made there. If the label further states '*mise en bouteille au château*' or '*mise en bouteille au domaine*' you can take it that the wine will have been bottled at the vineyard.

Food Content

The food we buy (whether tinned or fresh) must contain a certain amount of meat, fish, fruit or whatever, according to the way that food is described. The percentage of the most important ingredients is set down by law in terms of the Food Act. Some examples of the law in regard to food content are:

Meat Products
- Beef sausages should contain 50% beef.
- Cooked meat pies should contain at least 25% meat.

A minimum meat content is set down for a whole variety of products from sausages and hamburgers to Cornish pasties and potted .neats. This can vary from 10% to 95%, according to the product. The content of meat is subject to review from time to time. Local Trading Standards Offices can provide details of any new regulations.

Fish Products
- Fish paste must contain 70% fish.
- Fish cakes must contain 35% fish.

- Fish fingers have no minimum quantity.

Pastes and Spreads Pastes and pâtés must contain 70% meat or fish but it need not necessarily be of the kind specified on the label e.g. salmon spread must contain 70% fish, but not all the fish need be salmon.

Spreads must contain 70% meat or fish and all of that 70% must be the fish or meat named on the label.

Jams and Preserves Jams must contain at least 65% of soluble solids and have a minimum quantity of fruit, depending on the type:

- Strawberry jam must have at least 35% strawberries.
- Blackcurrant jam must have 25% fruit content.
- The words 'extra jam' are used to describe jam which contains extra fruit. Any jam bearing this description on the label must have a higher percentage of fruit than ordinary jam and the percentage, which varies according to the type of fruit, is set out in legislation.

Voluntary Codes Concerning Food Content

Over the years a number of codes of practice in regard to food have been agreed by the government and food manufacturers. They are purely voluntary and cannot be enforced in law. They do, however, represent the sort of standards which might well be accepted in any dispute and are broadly observed by firms.

Some of these codes are well observed for tinned products but not always so well for dried, packaged products. Tests have indicated that some packaged products contain only small percentages of meat.

The following are some examples of these voluntary codes.

Soup Content

- Tinned meat soups should contain at least 6% meat.
- Meat and vegetable soups should contain at least 3% meat.
- Dried soups should contain at least 3% meat.
- Dried meat and vegetable soups should contain at least 1.5% meat.

Biscuits

- A coconut biscuit should have coconut 'in a readily recognisable quantity'.
- A date biscuit must contain dates.
- A wine biscuit need not contain wine since wine indicates the use of the biscuit.
- 'Cheese assorted', 'cheddar assorted' biscuits need not contain cheese but the name of a particular cheese before the word 'biscuit' indicates cheese in the biscuit.

Special Rules

- Processed peas must not be referred to as 'fresh', 'garden' or 'green peas'.

- Tenderized meat must be called 'tenderized'.
- Liqueur chocolates must contain a 'significant' quantity of liqueur.

Listing By law the contents of food must be listed on the label – the ingredients must be listed in order of weight (the heaviest being given first) but only the actual percentage of those ingredients given 'special emphasis' need be given to conform with EEC rules. Added water need only be listed if it exceeds 5% of the total weight.

Required Fruit Content for Juices/Soft Drinks If something is described on the container as being fruit juice, drink, squash or whatever, then by law it must have a certain minimum fruit content according to that description.

- Anything described as 'natural fruit juice' or 'pure fruit juice' (from any type of fruit), must contain 100% juice.
- Any kind of 'fruit nectar' must contain a quantity of juice or puree and that minimum varies from 25% to 50% according to the fruit. For example: apple, orange or elderberry must have a minimum of 50%; peaches 45%; blackberries 40%; passion fruit 25% and so on. Each fruit has its own percentage and this is set down in the food regulations.
- A 'squash' made from a citrus fruit must have at least 25% fruit juice, but a 'squash' from a non-citrus fruit, such as strawberries, need only have a minimum of 10% fruit content.
- Barley water must have a minimum of 15% fruit juice – but if it is intended to be drunk without dilution, then it need only contain a minimum of 3% fruit content.
- Anything described as a 'crush' must have a minimum of 5% fruit with the exception of lime, which requires only 3%.
- Orangeade or any other fruit-flavoured drink so named need not actually have any fruit content at all.
- Something simply described as a 'drink' of any fruit flavour should have a minimum of 10% comminuted fruit, which means particles of the fruit as well as actual juice may be included in the percentage.

Vending machines So many soft drinks these days are sold though vending machines that the regulations cover them too. Any machine must display a notice in clear lettering and in a prominent position which gives the description of the drink available so that the customer will know whether he is getting a juice, a squash or whatever.

Fabric

When you buy a fabric today – whether it's by the metre to make up into clothes or soft furnishings or whether it is already made up into finished products – the law mostly requires the fibres to be identified.

If we know the composition of the fabric we are more likely to be able to consider its various qualities and for which purposes it will be suitable.

■ Often fabric sold by the roll will have the composition and the instructions for looking after it printed on the selvage.

■ On clothes, curtains, etc., the information will probably be contained on a woven label attached to the item. A typical label might read:

87% ACRYLIC 13% POLYESTER

LINING 100% acetate

Details of Care Symbols on Labels

The code basically consists of five symbols for the five care processes: washing, bleaching, ironing, dry cleaning and drying.

Washing Since 1986 the wash symbols have been changed. The three variables in the washing process (water temperature, agitation and spinning) are indicated by the tub symbols. Maximum water temperature is shown in degrees Celsius inside the tub. Agitation and spinning are both shown by the use of a bar or broken bar under the tub.

For the time being, while the new symbols are introduced, there will be explanatory words on the label such as 'wash as cotton'.

 means a 50° C wash with reduced mechanical action and short spin

 handwash (do not machine wash)

 do not wash

 Bleaching

 Chlorine bleach may be used

 Do not bleach

 Ironing

 Warm iron
An iron with one dot (.) means cool
An iron with three dots (. . .) means hot

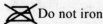 Do not iron

○ **Dry Cleaning**

(P) May be dry cleaned
Circle may contain letters A, P or F, depending on which solvent is suitable for the fabric. If the circle is underlined this indicates that special treatment is required and advice should be sought from a professional dry cleaner.

⊗ Do not dry clean

▢ **Drying**

⊡ Tumble drying beneficial

⊠ Do not tumble dry

More detailed information on the care of clothes labelling can be obtained from the Home Laundering Consultative Council.

Carpet Labelling

Just as fabric sold by the yard or made up into products has to be clearly marked with the fibre content, so every carpet requires labelling with a clear indication of its pile/yarn fibre content.

In addition to this there is a classification scheme run by the British Carpet Manufacturers' Association which covers pile carpets made by members. The new grading scheme based on BS7131 was launched in 1989. It includes independent checking of pile fibre weight and density, machine testing of a carpet's ability to keep its 'as new' look, random testing to maintain quality standards, and a room suitability guide shown on the label by pictures. Four grades are given: extra heavy, heavy, medium and light.

Labelling of Insecticides and Sprays

Any chemical used in insecticides and sprays for the home must be treated with caution. This why the labels of fly sprays usually carry some sort of instruction about keeping them away from food and children. Most fly killers and other pesticides are covered by regulations which control the classification, packaging and labelling of dangerous substances.

Labelling of Contact Lens Solutions

Those who wear contact lenses require special solutions to clean them and these solutions are subject to certain labelling regulations to ensure that specific information appears on the label, the box or in the literature.

The details must include:

- The batch the solution came from
- What the solution should be used for
- How it should be used
- The expiry date
- Time limit for use, once opened
- Which chemicals are included as disinfectants
- What percentage of solution the chemicals are
- Any necessary warnings

Labelling regulations were introduced in 1980 and bring these lens cleaners under the control of the Medicines Act.

All That Glitters May Not Be Gold!

Hallmarking of gold and silver items is one of the oldest forms of labelling or marking to provide information to the prospective purchaser. It started in the fourteenth century. The hallmark contains two separate elements. The first is the Assay Office Mark and there are four of these in the UK (London, Birmingham, Sheffield and Edinburgh) and the second is the Standard Mark which indicates the precious metal content.

Any jewellery made from platinum, silver or gold, must by law bear a hallmark, except in the case of gold which weighs less than 1g, silver less than 7.18g and platinum less than 5g.

To make sure that customers get all the relevant information in regard to gold and silver, a shop must display a card explaining what the hallmarks mean alongside any items on sale. This is a requirement under the Hallmarking Act 1973.

Goods which are silver plated, for example, must be labelled as such. A distinction must be made on labels between 'silver plate' which implies the article is made from solid silver and 'silver plated' which means the article is of electro-plated nickel silver.

Tyres

The information you require to make sure you have the correct tyre is found on the side of the tyre itself. You need to know what the numbers and letters mean. For example: 155R 12 76 S

155 means the tyre is 155 mm wide across its tread

R stands for radial, the type of construction

12 means this tyre fits on to a wheel rim of 12 inch diameter

76 is a load index, a code that relates to the maximum load the tyre can carry. In the case of 76 there is a maximum load of 400 kg

S is the speed symbol, indicating the maximum speed at which the tyre should be run at its maximum load. S – up to 112 mph; T – up to 118 mph; H – up to 130 mph; and V – up to 149 mph.

There will be a lot of other markings on the tyre relating to construction, composition and European and American regulations.

Weight

Most goods, whether they are prepacked (as most are these days), or weighed or measured on the spot, are very carefully controlled by legislation. This gives protection to the customer in two ways. Firstly, it ensures that weights and measures are accurate and, therefore, give value for money. Secondly, it means that shoppers must be provided, at counter level, with the relevant information on weight to enable comparison and assess value.

QUESTIONS TO ASK

Are you getting a full pound or pint?

Legislation in 1979 brought the 'average' system into weights and measures for prepacked goods from 1 January 1980. This is the system most widely used in Western countries. What it means is that those responsible for packing goods must ensure that the amount in the package is 'on average' what it says on the label but must never fall below a certain minimum quantity specified by law. So, sometimes you may get a few more peas in the tin than it declares on the label, sometimes a few less (but never less than that minimum quantity the law demands) . . . and generally you will get exactly the quantity the label states.

Local authority Trading Standards Officers enforce the law on weights and measures and they check on the quantity of prepacked goods on the packing line whether in factories or shops. Packers, traders and importers who break the law can be prosecuted.

Another of the duties of Trading Standards Officers is to carry out regular checks on all equipment which is used for weighing and measuring. This means that all such equipment must be verified and marked by an official, indicating it is accurate.

All equipment such as scales, weights, pint measures, rules and even petrol pumps are inspected, though some items such as fabric measuring instruments don't come within the regulations. Anyone with reason to suspect that they may not have received a full measure should report the matter to their local Trading Standards Office.

What are the rules about net and gross weight?

There are certain provisions under the Weights and Measures Act which deal with this point. For instance:

■ Tea, coffee and cocoa must be sold by **net** weight.

■ Meat can be sold by **gross** weight, providing that the wrapping paper used does not weigh more than 10g per kilogram of the gross weight. This does not apply to prepacked meat.

■ All prepacked packages must be marked with an indication of the net weight.

■ Fruit and vegetables can be sold either by net or gross weight – but, if sold gross, then there is a limit on the weight of the wrapper or container. A punnet which contains fruit for instance may be up to 12% of the gross weight, no more.

■ Fruit can be sold in single units if it's the easily counted kind.

■ If the weight of fish, meat or poultry is gross then the maximum weight of the wrapping included in that gross is set down by legislation.

Are there standard sizes for prepacked goods?

Yes, and this is part of a gradual harmonization of packet sizes throughout Europe. Detergent powders, for instance, are already standardized by manufacturers on a voluntary basis, at least as far as box size is concerned. But some standards are set down by law, e.g. prepacked tea must be sold in multiples of 25g, 50g, 250g, 500g, 750g, 1 kilogram, etc.

■ Pasta, salt, sugar, cereals, breakfast foods, oats, flour, dried vegetables, edible fats, jams, cereals and biscuits and certain other foods must be sold in prescribed weights.

■ Cocoa and chocolate powders can only be sold in weights of 50g, 75g, 125g, 250g, 500g, 750g or 1kg units.

■ Chocolate bars are to be sold only in weights of 85g, 100g, 125g, 150g, 200g, 250g, 300g, 400g or 500g.

■ Coal and other solid fuels sold in bags must be sold either in units of 7lb, 14lb, 28lb, 56lb, 1/2 cwt, 112lb, 140lb or multiples of 112lb, or in 25kg or 50kg units, or multiples of 50kg.

What is Euro sizing?

Euro sizing comprises standard pack sizes which manufacturers of a particular type of product all use, making it easier for the shopper to compare one brand with another in terms of value for money. For instance, most washing powders – whichever company makes them – are marketed in Euro sizes. E1, E2, E3, E10 are the most commonly found packs on the supermarket shelves. E1 is the smallest size and the larger sizes are multiples of it. So E10 which is the usual largest size of washing powder is in fact 10 times larger than an E1 size by volume. There is also an E20 size now for some brands.

These Euro sizes, however, are basically describing the size of the container rather than the actual weight of the contents inside it. It is not likely, though, that there will be any marked variation in actual weight between one brand E10 pack and another and any slight difference would be accounted for by a difference in density of the particular powder.

The E10 large pack will normally contain 2.8kg (6.17lb).

Can the weight marked be either imperial or metric?

Metrication has not progressed as well as originally planned, which means that while some foods are completely metricated in terms of package marking, others are still using a dual system giving both metric and imperial weights, while others, such as honey and jam, are still sold in prescribed imperial quantities.

The legislation provides for all three – specifying some foods which must be packed in metric quantities only, some which may be packed in either imperial or metric and others which can only be packed in imperial quantities. Those recently switched to metric will be marked METRIC PACK and have the imperial also given and indeed the shopper will find dual marking fairly common.

What does drained weight mean?

This is sometimes given on such things as tins of fruit and it can be very useful in terms of comparing the value of one product against another. It means quite simply the weight of the fruit or other 'solid' ingredients without the weight of the fruit syrup or their liquid.

How much wine can one expect to get in a carafe or glass?

Until the introduction of the Weights and Measures (Sale of Wine) Order 1976 there was no way of judging how much wine a carafe served in a restaurant was likely to contain – in fact it could vary from one litre to half a litre! No indication of the quantity was to be found either on the menu or the container itself. However, since the legislation came into force in 1977 carafes of wine must come in one of these quantities:

1/4 litre, 1/2 litre, 3/4 litre, 1 litre or alternatively 1/2 pint or 1 pint.

And as a further guide to help customers, a written note giving clear details of the quantities on sale is required. This can be on the wine list, menu or displayed in some other form but these regulations cover only carafes of wine and not glasses of wine.

Anyone who orders a carafe and finds no indication in the restaurant or cafe of the quantity being sold should report the matter to their local Trading Standards or Consumer Protection Office.

Two glass sizes, 75ml and 125ml, are standard measures for wine in pubs and wine bars.

Bar Codes in Supermarkets

The increasing use of electronics has brought laser beams and electronic checkouts to many supermarkets, DIY stores and other large stores.

The **Laser Scanning System** has brought us bar codes on tins, packets and bottles.

These codes appear on most products sold in groceries and supermarkets and many other items such as books are coded in a similar way. Most department stores use price tags which include their own codes for scanning at the cash desk.

With this new system the checkout assistant no longer has to read the price on the product and ring it upon the register. Instead the bar code is scanned when it is passed across a laser beam. The laser is linked to a computer, the price is relayed back to the checkout and displayed electronically so that the customer can see the price. One advantage to the consumer is that you get a detailed printout at the checkout. Not only is the price of the item given but the name of it is printed alongside, for example:

DB DOG FOOD .30
BREAD .50
BUTTER .49

One disadvantage for consumers is that prices of individual items would not necessarily be marked on tins and packets, so to make sure you're not charged what the shelf label says it may be necessary to jot it down on the shopping list as you go along.

QUESTIONS TO ASK

What does the bar code mean?

The bar code has two parts. One is a 13-digit number and the other consists of corresponding lines of varying thicknesses above the numbers. The machine in the back shop can 'read' this and come up with a price. The first two numbers in the code indentify the country of origin – 50 is Britain. The next five numbers identify the manufacturer, the next five tell the computer what the product is and the last number is an accuracy check.

There is an international formula for numbering, agreed by the European Article Numbering Association.

How are products identified?

This is up to each individual manufacturer and they are the ones normally responsible for coding items, arranging the second set of five numbers as they like. The codes are then passed on to retailers and they in turn use the numbers to identify the items in their computer file.

Could the customer be wrongly charged?

This could happen if, for instance, the price held by the computer is different from the one displayed on the shelf.

The only way shoppers would know about this is if they noted down the prices of all the items on their shopping list and then compared those with the prices on the printout bill. In this context it is worth bearing in mind that it is an offence under the Consumer Protection Act to indicate a lower price than the one that actually applies. To protect the customer, guidelines operate among retailers – for instance, the prices on the computer will be increased only when the store is closed thus cutting out any possibility of a price increase while the customer is actually shopping. However, there have been a number of instances where the price on the computer has been increased but the shelf price has remained lower. Prosecutions by Trading Standards Officers have resulted in large fines and adverse publicity for the stores involved. This should ensure stricter control by retailers in future but it pays to be vigilant.

Unit Pricing

How can you possibly decide whether a 396g (14oz) tin of beans at 15p is better value than a 439g (15½oz) tin at 17p? Unless you happen to have a particular aptitude for figures or a pocket calculator in your shopping basket, it can be quite impossible to decide which offers best value for money.

Unit pricing provides the obvious solution. This way, the price per unit of measurement, whether it's a pound, kilo, litre or other unit, is clearly indicated on the label alongside the full price. This method of pricing was compulsory in many European countries for some time before it was introduced to Britain. It is now seen here, to a limited extent only, as a result of various orders made under the Weights and Measures Act and the Prices Act. These relate mostly to fresh foodstuffs rather than dried or tinned.

Foods which Must be Unit Priced by Law

■ Meat – whether it's fresh, chilled or frozen.
■ Fish – some types of fresh, chilled or frozen.
■ Fruit and vegetables e.g. the individual price of an orange would be indicated.
■ Cheese – if not prepacked then the price per pound must be shown and if prepacked then both the price per pound (the unit price) and the selling price of the pack must be shown on it.

Trade Descriptions/Advertising

The Trade Descriptions Act was hailed as the Consumer's Charter when it was introduced. It aims to prevent consumers being misled by false descriptions of goods or services. In the case of goods, anyone who in the course of trade or business applies a false trade description to any goods or who supplies or offers to supply any goods which are falsely described is guilty of an offence. They can be prosecuted as a result.

So, what comes under the heading of 'trade description'?
■ Any indication of quantity or size – for instance 'will cover at least ten square yards'.
■ Method of manufacture – e.g. 'handmade' or 'prepacked'.
■ Composition – 'stainless steel', 'leather'.
■ Fitness for purpose. If something is described as 'waterproof' then it must be.

- Particular characteristics claimed for a product, e.g. that a garment is 'drip dry', 'colour fast' or a container is 'unbreakable'.
- The name given to a product. Diamonds, for instance, must be the genuine article and not zircons.
- The mileage displayed on the mileometer of a car.
- The name, place and date of manufacture.
- Any claims about the testing or approval of the goods.
- Pictures and illustrations indicating contents or use of product.

It is not only written statements which are covered by the act. If the description is given to the customer by word of mouth, or it is in a catalogue, brochure, invoice, voucher, package or in an advertisement it is subject to the same legislation.

A typical complaint under the Trade Descriptions Act which would be referred by a consumer to the Trading Standards Office might be that a man bought a multi-purpose saw in his local do-it-yourself shop. On the front of the box was a coloured picture showing very clearly the saw cutting through what appeared to be an ordinary house brick. It was only after the chap had paid for the saw and got it home and opened it that he found a printed slip of paper stating quite clearly that the manufacturer did not recommend the saw for cutting bricks.

Action would be taken on such a complaint where it seemed the customer was being misled by the description on the box. In this case the 'description' was the picture and it was obviously at odds with the actual use to which the product could be put.

Advertising

Descriptions given in advertisements must not be in any way false or misleading because they come under the umbrella of the Trade Descriptions Act. Other legislation can affect advertising claims, too.
- The Food Act does not allow any advertisements which might mislead consumers as to the substance or quality of food or drugs or as to the nutritional value of food. This includes many products which make claims regarding 'slimming' properties.
- The Food Labelling Regulations say that any claims made must be true and not phrased in a way that could mislead, e.g. claims that certain products 'replace energy' could be misleading because all food and drink does that to some degree! 'Tonic' properties in any product are also not permitted.
- Under the Medicines Act there are regulations which ban advertisements which allege cures for certain diseases. Advertisements of any medicines which are only available on prescription are also banned.

■ The Consumer Credit Act 1974 contains certain constraints in advertising. Claims such as 'interest free' cannot be made unless the total amount payable does not exceed the cash price and any credit or hire advertisements which are false or misleading are banned.

The Advertising Standards Authority

This is an organization set up by the advertising trade. It has its own code of practice to protect consumers from untrue or misleading claims in advertising matter and it will consider complaints from members of the public in regard to this. It has no legal force.

FOUR

PRICING AND PAYING

The shopper is faced with a considerable choice of prices in the High Street. Different brands of the same product can carry widely varying price tags – there are 'special offers' and 'bargain offers', not to mention sales and claims about reductions in the manufacturers' recommended price.

It can often be difficult to know just which offer really is giving good value and which only sounds as though it is.

This is where the Consumer Protection Act 1987 and the Code of Practice for Traders on Price Indications provides reassurance. It is a criminal offence to give consumers a misleading price indication about goods, services, accommodation (including the sale of new homes) or facilities. It applies however the price indication is given – whether in a TV or press advert, in a catalogue or leaflet, on notices, price tickets or shelf-edge marking in stores, or if it is given by word of mouth.

Sales

'Formerly £15 – now reduced to £7'. Such a price tag on a dress certainly makes it look like a very good bargain. But how do we know that the dress was ever actually on sale for £15?

The Code of Practice gives guidance to retailers that
- the previous price should be the **last** price in the previous six months
- it should have been available at that price for 28 consecutive days in the previous six months
- the previous price should have applied for that period at the **same** shop where the reduced price is now offered.

If the circumstances of the price reduction don't fit these conditions the retailer should display a specific explanation, such as 'these goods were on sale here at the higher price from 1 February to 26 February'.

Does a reduced price mean reduced rights?

No. Your rights under the Sale of Goods Act are exactly the same as when goods are offered for sale at the full price. Whatever you buy must be exactly as described on the label or the package. So if the picture on the box shows a hair dryer, and what you have actually bought turns out to be a set of heated rollers, you are entitled to take it back to the shop and ask for a refund.

The product must be fit for the purpose – so if the shoes with pounds off their price are supposed to be waterproof then they must be. The product must also be of merchantable quality, so anything in the sale which you later discover doesn't work can be returned and a refund demanded.

'No refunds given on sale goods in any circumstances'

If you come across such a notice, it has no effect at all on your basic right to get your money back should the goods prove to be defective. Moreover, it is a criminal offence for a shop to display such a notice, so report it to the local Trading Standards or Consumer Protection Office.

Shopsoiled or damaged items offered at a reduced price must be clearly marked as such. If you are aware that they do have slight defects or are stained then, of course, you cannot take them back to the shop and claim a refund on the basis of a fault you should have spotted.

'Seconds', 'substandard' or 'imperfect' goods should be considered very carefully. These terms should not mean that the item is in any sense useless, but it is as well to be aware that the quality will be lower than usual and you cannot claim a refund for what is a cosmetic fault.

Misleading Prices

The Code of Practice for Traders on Price Indications also gives retailers guidance on
- making a series of reductions
- introductory offers, after-sale or after promotion prices
- comparisons with prices related to different circumstances
- comparisons with 'Recommended Retail Price' or similar
- pre-printed prices, references to value or worth, sales or special events and free offers
- the actual price given to the consumer (including non-optional extras, postage, VAT etc.)

- how to deal with prices which later become misleading such as those in magazines, brochures and catalogues where the price increases after a period of time

Anyone who comes across a price indication they feel might be illegal because it seems intended to mislead, should report the matter to their local Trading Standards or Consumer Protection Office. These are the authorities who have the power to enforce current legislation.

If price comparisons which appear misleading are part of an advertisement, then also get in touch with the Advertising Standards Authority.

Trading Stamps

Intended to attract customers by giving them a 'discount' on goods they buy, trading stamps can be exchanged for either money or goods. If goods being sold in two shops are of exactly similar size and quality and one of the shops offers stamps with the goods then this may indeed give better value to the customer. It may be difficult, though, for the customer to establish beyond any doubt that the goods are the same – so always check carefully before being tempted by stamps.

Rights in Regard to Stamps:
- All stamps issued must state their cash redemption value and all those of 25p or over may be redeemed for cash on demand.
- Shops must display a notice stating clearly how many stamps a customer is entitled to.
- All establishments offering stamps must keep a supply of stamp-saving books or catalogues.
- As a result of the Supply of Goods (Implied Terms) Act 1973 a customer has the same rights when redeeming trading stamps as when buying goods in the ordinary way. Goods you receive in exchange must be of merchantable quality and fit for their purpose.

Excluded!

Stamp or token schemes produced and distributed by one shop or one manufacturer for its own use as opposed to a trading stamp company, are not covered by the legislation. Nor are the 'dividend stamps' offered by the various co-operative societies.

Free Offers

The idea of something for nothing appeals to most of us and so one form of sales promotion is the 'free offer'. There are conditions to watch out for, however. The Code of Practice gives guidance to retailers that:

■ they should make clear to you, at the time of the offer for sale, exactly what they will have to buy to get the 'free offer'

■ if they give an indication of the cash value of the 'free offer' and it is not the shop's current price for the product, more explanation should be given

■ they should make clear any conditions of the offer giving the main points with the price indication and where you can get more details before committing yourself to buy

■ they should **not** claim an offer is free if there are additional charges not normally made, the price is inflated or that it would be reduced if you didn't take up the offer.

Law Lords' Decision

A case concerning World Cup coins set the principle of 'no redress in free gifts'. Five law lords decided that since an item is given away there is no contract of sale and therefore no protection for the customer under the Sale of Goods Act.

Money-off Coupons

Some 7.5 billion coupons are distributed in the UK every year – some on packets, some in printed advertisements and a growing number delivered through the letterbox by the postman. The idea is to offer the consumer a reduced price in the hope that existing customers will have an incentive to continue buying that particular brand and also to tempt new customers into trying the brand in preference to the one they normally buy.

QUESTIONS TO ASK

What if the retailer won't accept the coupon?

This usually only happens in small shops, but if it does there's not a lot the shopper can do. The wording on the coupons is part of the advertisement and is subject to the Advertising Code of Practice. But no complaints about coupons being refused have yet been upheld because the wording is only to be taken in 'general' terms. Just because one or two shops won't accept the coupon it does not mean that the claim on the coupon is either misleading or invalid. The manufacturers can argue that even if only 95% of shops accept coupons this is reasonable and the advertising body accepts that.

Anyone who has a limited choice of shops or lives in an isolated area and can't get a shop to accept the coupon should write to the manufacturer of the product. Food Manufacturers' Federation members have a general policy of sending a postal order, a voucher or something similar to someone in these circumstances, to make sure they do get the benefit of the money-off coupons and won't suffer just because the shops are not so accessible to them.

For how long is a coupon valid?

The Food Manufacturers' Federation together with the Institute of Sales Promotion and the British Multiple Retailers' Association have worked out a set of guidelines for coupons used in sales promotions. One says that 'coupons printed on a pack should have no closing date applied to them, with the exception of goods carrying date stamps'. Where a closing date is applied in coupons in publications or delivered door to door 'the date should be clearly and conspicuously marked on the front face using copy "valid until . . .".'

Price Increases: If you are ordering goods rather than buying them on the spot, it's wise to do this on the basis of a 'fixed price' otherwise you might find yourself in for a shock when the goods are eventually delivered. Often the price of new stock has increased compared to the model which has been in the showroom for some time and which now costs more.

Always ask exactly how much when the assistant says the price may have gone up a little.

If no possibility of an increase is mentioned – then ask anyway.

Dual Pricing: Occasionally you may come across a shop (perhaps at sale time) or garage, which charges one price to customers paying cash and another higher charge to those paying by credit card. Most credit card companies have arrangements with traders which do not allow them any freedom to impose surcharges. This practice has been investigated by the Monopolies and Mergers Commission who have recommended that the credit card companies should not restrict retailers in this way.

Value Added Tax (VAT)

Value Added Tax was introduced on 1 April 1973 and is applied at whatever rate is fixed by the government. It applies both to goods and services but some things do not involve a tax charge to the consumer. Most food, books, newspapers and fuel are zero rated, as are children's clothes. Insurance, the postal service, education and health are exempt.

The Code of Practice for Traders on Price Indications states that **all** price indications given to private consumers, by whatever means, should include VAT.

In the case of professional fees the price (including estimates) should generally include VAT where the fee is based on an as-yet-unknown sum of money, for example on the sale price of a house, the fee quoted should either include VAT or make it clear that VAT has to be paid. For example: 'Fee of 1.5% of purchase price plus VAT at 15%'.

For building work, estimates should either include VAT in the price or indicate with equal prominence the amount or rate of VAT payable in addition to the basic figure.

If VAT is shown as a separate amount your attention should be drawn to the fact that the amount of VAT payable will vary if any provisional sum in the estimate varies.

Does the shop have to sell at the marked price?

The answer is no. If the shop accepts your offer to buy then the price he charges must be the price displayed (under the Consumer Protection Act it is an offence to mark goods with a price below which they are for sale), but the shopkeeper is within his rights to **refuse to sell you the goods** either at the price marked, or indeed at any price!

Even in a self-service store all the shopper can legally do is 'make an offer' for goods on display and that offer is only accepted when the shop takes cash from the customer. This also means that until he has actually paid for them the shopper is quite entitled to change his mind and put goods back on the shelf.

Paying

Once you've made your purchases, how do you pay for them? For smaller items at least, cash, in the form of notes and coins, looks like being popular for some time to come with an increasing number of cash dispensers at banks providing easy access to it. Cheques, of course, are another widely accepted way of paying for goods, particularly when payment is being sent by post. But for purchases over £50 they can present problems since that's the limit of your cheque-card guarantee. Then there are a number of credit facilities which allow the customer to pay by instalments, with the credit supplier charging interest on the purchase price.

Cash

If you decide to pay for goods or services with cash in the form of coins or notes, it may be as well to remember that there are laws governing 'legal tender'. Legal tender simply means coins or notes which a trader must by law, accept. He is not obliged to accept all kinds or amounts!

- Bronze coins are only legal tender up to an amount of 20 pence.
- 5 pence, 10 pence and 20 pence coins are legal tender up to a total of £5.
- 50 pence coins are legal tender only up to £10 worth.
- Bank notes up to any amount are acceptable in England and Wales, but in Scotland only Bank of England notes are, in fact, legal tender (not Scottish banknotes).

And if you have ever wondered if those buses which demand 'exact fares' only and whose drivers refuse to give change to passengers, are legally entitled to do so – the answer is an emphatic yes. In fact, no trader has any legal obligation to give a customer change – but the customer does have an obligation to hand over the correct amount by way of payment.

Credit Cards

The first card was introduced by one of the clearing banks in 1966, other banks followed and today millions of people in Britain use them. There are three issued by the different banks – Barclaycard, Access and Trustcard and they all work on much the same basis. You don't need to have a bank account to get a credit card but most cardholders probably do.

The customer is given a credit limit and can buy goods or services up to that total. An average credit limit is £300. Every month you get a statement showing what you owe and the minimum amount you are required to repay (by law either £5 or 5% of the total owing whichever happens to be the greater). The statement also has the repayment dates on it. Twenty-five days are allowed for payment and if you pay within that time no interest is payable.

After the 25-day period, interest is charged monthly at a fixed rate on a daily basis. The true annual rate can be anything from 25% to 30% depending on current interest rates. Different card companies have slightly different methods of working out interest which often makes direct comparison difficult.

Cash advances can be taken out with a credit card. Credit cards can be used to obtain money abroad and to buy goods from any retail outlet.

Advantages:

■ Convenient and flexible. Can be absolutely free if you pay within the 25 days and fairly cheap if you pay within a few months (but can be costly if you leave the debt running).

■ More useful than cheques for items costing over £50.

■ You can use cards to buy things over the phone or by mail simply by quoting the card number.

■ Certain safeguards for the customer. If goods bought by credit card costing more than £100 turn out to be faulty then the card company has equal responsibility with the retailer for putting things right.

■ If a company goes out of business or bankrupt and you have made a payment of £100 or more for goods or services direct to them by credit card, then the credit company will make good your loss.

■ In the case of a lost or stolen credit card, providing the card company is alerted to the loss as soon as possible, you are only liable in law for £25 if someone else has used the card fraudulently, and most companies do not make the cardholder pay even that amount.

Disadvantages:

■ If you don't pay off credit quickly it can cost more than, say, a bank overdraft.

■ Not every shop or retail outlet will take a credit card as payment.

■ Credit cards encourage one to spend more and more, as some people regard 'plastic' money as less real than cash or cheques.

■ Using them for cash withdrawals can be very costly.

Cash Replacement Cards

These are not credit cards as defined by consumer law and there are only two of them in the UK – Diners' Club and American Express. They simply allow one to spend without actually carrying money around in one's pocket. The full amount due must be settled each month – they are not geared to credit. The cardholder pays an initial membership fee and on top of that, an annual subscription.

They can be useful for those who travel abroad a lot. They do not offer the same protection as credit cards.

Payment Card Linked to Bank: Electronic Funds Transfer (EFT)

Some of the major banks have introduced a 'debit' card which can be used for purchases of any price subject to funds being available in the buyer's bank account. There is no delay as in a cheque being cleared as the sum is immediately deducted from the buyer's current account by electronic transfer at the point of sale. What happens is that a customer hands over a plastic card (similar to a credit card) and it is put into a slot in a special machine at the cash desk. The customer's personal number, his bank account number and the total of his purchases is punched in at the point of sale and the details will be registered both in the customer's and the shop's bank accounts.

Store Credit Cards

The new version of the most familiar credit accounts shops provide for customers. Plastic cards are now issued which can be used only in the store issuing them. There are over 2,500,000 store cards in the UK. Three main types of store cards are available.

Monthly account cards mean that you will be sent a statement on the same date each month and you have to pay the mount owing. Normally no credit is allowed but if you do pay it off late then you may well be charged interest.

Option account cards give one the option of paying off the whole amount shown on the statement or of only paying off part of it. It is similar to the bank credit card system in that you must by law pay off either £5 or 5% of the total, whichever is the greater. Interest is charged on the outstanding balance.

Budget account cards are the most popular today. The customer pays a minimum amount each month into the account and can then borrow up to so many times that amount – usually 24 times the amount you pay in. Normally the minimum monthly payment one could make would be £5.

Advantages:
- They're useful if you buy a lot of goods in the same shop and an account does allow you to buy bigger items for which you may not be able to afford to pay cash.
- You can pay off more per month when you have money to spare and reduce your credit interest charges.
- Under the Consumer Credit Act as 'credit tokens' they give the customer double protection in case of faulty goods. Both the finance company issuing the card and the supplier of the goods can be liable for putting things right – if they cost £100 or more.

Disadvantages:
- They tend to restrict your buying to the one shop.

■ Interest rates vary from one shop to another – even two shops with a card run by the same finance house can offer quite different interest rates.

■ Unless you make your monthly payments by standing order some shops will charge a higher than normal interest rate.

■ It could be argued that you are simply giving the shop an interest-free loan.

Credit Balance

There are a few stores which give you interest on the credit balance in your account. One even provides the customer with a special cheque book with cheques already made payable to the store. The interest rate varies according to current interest rates. The advantage of this system is that you are getting a small return for your money.

Longer Term Credit

If you pay for something by regular instalments it can ease the financial strain on the budget quite considerably, and perhaps release your capital for those emergencies which invariably crop up. There are various credit options available on a longer term basis. The first and probably the most familiar form of buying on the 'never never' is hire purchase.

Hire Purchase (HP): Under this arrangement, the goods that you buy with a loan either from the trader or from a finance company do not become your property until the last instalment is paid. So the emphasis here must be on the word 'hiring'.

If you fall behind with payments then the goods could be taken back by the hirer (in effect the firm supplying the finance), but if you have paid more than one third of the total payments at the time of your default, then the hirer can only take the goods back if he gets a court order which enables him to do so.

■ Since the goods are not yours, you cannot, of course, sell them while you are still paying for them.

■ If you decide that you do not want the goods or cannot afford them you can return them. But you may have to pay half the total purchase price (the statutory minimum you can be required to pay) and that is in addition to returning the goods.

■ The rate of interest is generally fixed and will not change throughout the duration of the agreement. So if you take on an HP agreement when interest rates are low, you could be lucky! If rates increase again, yours doesn't.

■ If under 18 a customer will almost certainly be asked to give the name of a 'guarantor'. That person will guarantee to pay the instalments if the customer defaults and the 'guarantor' has a legal responsibility to do so. **Never act as guarantor without giving it a great deal of thought.**

■ This can sometimes be a fairly expensive method of getting credit in terms of interest charged. So check the annual percentage rate (see below) very carefully.

Conditional Sale Agreements: This is very similar to HP because the same basis operates, i.e. the goods only become one's property when the last instalment is paid to the finance company. In this instance one is not 'hiring' but 'getting the use of' the goods while paying.

Credit Sale: This is easily confused with HP because the agreement looks very much the same and the loan is paid off by instalments. The big difference is that with a credit sale agreement, the customer owns the goods right from the moment of making the purchase. This means that even if you default on the payments the finance company cannot take the goods away from you. They can only sue you for outstanding monies.

With a credit sale you could sell the goods if you wanted to, but you'd probably have to pay off any outstanding loan. Usually the repayment period is shorter than with a hire purchase agreement – anything from six months to two years.

Finance Company Personal Loan: Car dealers, gas and electricity boards and so on may offer to set up this sort of loan when the purchase is a big one. Terms vary from one company to another and it can work out quite expensively. Normally the loan is paid back over a period of up to three years. You own the goods right from the start and the interest rate is fixed throughout the repayment period.

Consumer Protection in Credit Deals

Those who want to borrow money for a purchase must, by law, be told the truth about the terms they are being offered. This allows the customer to compare the cost of one kind of credit with another or that being offered by one shop with that being offered by another. Credit charges and interest must always be worked out by the same process to ensure uniformity and allow accurate comparison. The Annual Percentage Rate (APR) came on to the scene in 1980 as a result of the Consumer Credit Act. The APR is the true cost of credit and includes all costs which make up the credit charge.

The APR must be shown on cards in shop windows offering goods on credit terms, in newspaper advertisements, handbills and so on, even in televison ads. Traders must give customers who ask written information about the credit terms being offered. That writen information, or quotation as it is commonly called has to give these details:

- the deposit
- the amount, number and frequency of payments
- the total credit price – everything included
- the APR
- the price if you were to pay cash

How do you work out the true rate of interest? If you borrow £100 and pay back £110 over 12 months with a payment every month, you are not actually paying an interest rate of 10%. This is because you are reducing the amount of the loan every month but the interest rate doesn't take account of that; you're being charged interest as though you still owed £100. So paying back £110 in fact represents a true interest rate of 19%. To work out what the APR is, you simply multiply the annual flat rate (10% in the example above) by 1.8 if you are to make quarterly payments or 1.9 if you pay by monthly instalments. The Office of Fair Trading produces 'Consumer Credit Tables' and Trading Standards Departments usually have copies.

Credit Reference Agencies

If you ask for credit and are refused it you will want to know why. It's possible that the firm checked you out with a credit reference agency. There have been mistakes in these agency files such as names being mixed up. So anyone who has been turned down for credit is entitled to ask the shop or firm for the name and address of any credit reference agency used. Then they can write off to the agency and ask for details of their file. If any details are incorrect the person can correct them. This costs £1. If the shop will not supply this information verbally, then the customer should put the request in writing. Note that this right of request only operates up to 28 days after the end of the negotiations to obtain credit. However you can write directly to any credit reference agency at any time enclosing your £1 and asking for details of your file.

Liability for Faulty Goods

In the case of HP, Conditional Sale and Credit Sale agreements the finance company is responsible for goods being as described, of merchantable quality and fit for a particular purpose.

Where the finance is a personal loan agreement, a credit card or store card and there is a business relationship between the retailer and finance company, both are liable for faulty or wrongly described goods as long as the cash price is £100 or more.

Copies of the Agreement

It is essential to read through any agreement very carefully before signing because, in general, you must abide by its terms. If possible, ask for a copy to take home and read through before signing. However, the customer is entitled by law to a copy of the signed agreement. If it is not available to him on the spot then it must be sent to him within seven days.

Look for the box on the agreement pointing out that you should only sign if you wish to be bound by the terms of the agreement!

If someone refuses to give you a copy of a credit agreement then it is unenforceable. Of course, as soon as a copy is supplied the agreement is in force – the failure to supply a copy does not cancel it.

If you lose your copy you can write to the owner or the seller of the goods and he is bound to send you a copy (he is free to charge 50p for doing so).

If you are not sure exactly how many payments you have made or what exactly your balance is then you are entitled to ask, in writing, for a statement showing the amount already paid, the amount still to be paid and any arrears.

Credit Agreements Signed 'Off Trade Premises'

If you sign an agreement on business premises – i.e. in the shop where you are buying the goods – then you are legally bound by the terms of any credit contract once it has been signed by or on behalf of the finance company. However, if you sign it 'off trade premises' – for instance where goods are being sold or in your own home – then the law allows a 'cooling-off period' which gives you time to re-consider and cancel the agreement should you wish.

This five-day cooling-off period starts from the day immediately after the customer gets his copy by post, not from the day he signs the agreement. Within that five-day period the customer has the legal right to cancel the agreement.

These various protections given to those buying goods on credit come under the Consumer Credit Act. They apply only to credit agreements where the amount borrowed is more than £50 and up to £15,000.

Some Pertinent Points about Paying – Cash or Credit

Cancellation of Cash Contracts Signed at Home

If a sales person calls at your house or workplace uninvited, or after an uninvited telephone call, and you agree to buy goods or a service costing over £35, you have rights to cancel. The sales person should give you written notice of cancellation rights at the time the sale is made otherwise the firm cannot enforce the contract. You have seven days to cancel.

Deposits

In most credit agreements for purchases, one is required to pay a percentage of the price by way of a cash deposit. However, there is another kind of 'deposit' which is not necessarily associated with credit facilities. This is when you hand over a certain amount of money as a sign of good faith in regard to a purchase. It may be that:

■ You haven't definitely decided whether you will buy an item in a shop – you want some time to think about it and would like the shop to set the article aside until you do decide. In this case, provided you return within the time limit agreed with the shop, and decide not to buy, you are still entitled to get the deposit back. However, that entitlement depends on your having initially agreed with the trader that your deposit would be returnable. It's always best to get that in writing, to prevent any dispute or misunderstanding.

■ It may be that you purchase a suite of furniture or a carpet from a store, which is not available from stock, but has to be ordered. In this case a deposit may be asked for and it would not usually be a returnable one. And in this case, make sure that a time limit is set for the goods ordered to be delivered and stipulate that if the delivery is not on time the deposit will be returned to you. Get this written on to the order and keep a copy of it.

■ Sometimes there is what is called a 'returnable deposit' on goods. This is usually when you have hired something for use – perhaps a tool or even glasses – and the deposit is by way of an insurance for the supplier.

Sale or Return

A system often used when shopping for food and drink for a party. Valuable when you don't know exactly how much you will need. The shop charges you for whatever quantity you order and take away, but there is an agreement that you will get a refund on everything you do not use and take back to the shop. Make sure that a date of return is agreed and that anything not used is actually returned by that date otherwise the shop would be entitled to charge you.

Paying Interest on Unpaid Bills

Lots of people pay things like milk and newspapers by monthly account, and if bills are not paid promptly some shops will actually charge 'interest' on the amount outstanding. They are only entitled legally to do this if it has been made very clear to you in advance and, therefore, forms part of your contract with them. Anyone who gets a bill with interest added on to it in this fashion does not have to pay it unless the interest was part of the terms of business accepted in the first place.

Receipts for Payment

If a bill is paid by cheque then many people are quite happy to accept that it acts as a receipt and require no further proof of payment. Some bills, such as electricity, have a box to tick if a receipt is required. It was once true that if a bill came to £2 or more, one was legally entitled to a receipt because stamp duty had to be paid. However in 1971 this stamp duty was abolished and so it has not been possible, since that date, to insist on getting a receipt.

Normally, if you buy something in a shop then you do get a receipt – even if it is only a print-out from the cash register with the shop's name and address on it – and this can be useful in case of a complaint later. If it is absolutely essential to have a receipt then arrange it with the shop or firm in advance so that it then becomes part of your contract with them.

If you find a notice displayed in a shop stating 'No refunds given without receipts', which tends to suggest that you must have a receipt before a complaint about goods can be dealt with, report the trader to your local Trading Standards Office, because such notices are illegal. Your rights are in no way affected in relation to defective goods if you can't produce a receipt.

FIVE

▇▇▇

PROTECTION

Buying any product can be a chancy business at the best of times. We can never be absolutely sure that we have made a wise choice and spent our money well. As someone said as long ago as the 1600s, 'A buyer needs a hundred eyes.'

But there are, fortunately, various ways in which a consumer is provided with protection in regard to his or her purchases. Some of these area matter of law, some agreed purely on a voluntary basis, while some relate to the actual goods and others give some indication of the reliability and standards of the place of purchase.

Trade Associations

A trade association is a group of firms in the same field – whether it's footwear or furniture – who join together, their prime concern being to protect the interests of their member companies. However, it is undoubtedly in the interests of an association to build up and preserve a good reputation with their customers and many (at least 20) have drawn up voluntary Codes of Practice which, in their own way, protect the customer.

These codes came about as a result of the Fair Trading Act which says that the Director-General of Fair Trading has a duty 'to encourage relevant associations to prepare codes of practice for guidance in safeguarding and promoting the interests of consumers'. They are all voluntary, but most of the trade associations do their best to make sure the terms of their codes are observed because, of course, each code is monitored by the Office of Fair Trading (OFT). The aim is to ensure that the customer gets a fair deal and so the codes generally offer two things.

■ They set down guidelines of good practice in regard to the customer that should result in better service.

■ If things go wrong, the trade asociation concerned provides a conciliation or arbitration service which attempts to settle any dispute between customer and retailer. Such a service is normally free. And, if things still don't work out, one's normal legal rights are not in any way affected.

■ **WARNING:** Don't assume that these trade associations will prove to be the answer to every problem that crops up in regard to purchases. Some seem to process complaints more efficiently than others and many consumer organizations feel that because these Codes of Practice are voluntary, they are not very effective. But it's still worthwhile shopping where you see a symbol which shows that the trader belongs to the relevant trade association because it can afford that little extra protection and provide another avenue of complaint.

Of course, to take advantage of these codes you must first know what their terms are. And, unfortunately, almost without exception, shops which work to a code do **not** supply copies of it on the counter for customers to read in order to establish their rights before buying!

Why not? There's no satisfactory answer to that one, although some traders have been known to say they simply haven't the room to stock lots of leaflets. Others say that, if a customer asks, they will be shown a copy which is kept on the premises – though traders don't display a notice to this effect!

The best plan is to get leaflets issued by the Office of Fair Trading on the various codes and read them at your leisure before you go shopping. Ask for them at Citizens Advice Bureaux, Trading Standards Departments or write directly to the OFT.

Some Points from Codes of Practice

Furniture: This code was drawn up in 1978 and covers most of the big multiples and the smaller retailers.

■ Any labels on furniture should be very clear and include not only the price (with VAT inclusive) but also details of what the item is made of, its measurements and any special properties (if it is covered in a stain-resistant fabric, for instance).

■ Delivery dates must be accurate rather than wildly optimistic and, if the date is more than one month ahead, then it must be put down in writing for the customer. If the delivery date is not going to be met, then the retailer should alert the customer as soon as possible. If the new date does not suit, then the customer should be given the chance to cancel and have the deposit refunded. (See also page 79 for further information on delivery dates.)

- The price you pay must be the one pertaining when you ordered the goods. If a higher price is anticipated, for any reason, then the customer must be advised of this at the time of ordering. If the VAT rate increases after the order is placed it's usual for the customer to have to pay the extra involved.
- Staff in furniture shops ought to be trained sufficiently to advise on their products and to deal with any complaints which might arise.
- There is a complaints procedure, a conciliation procedure and an arbitration scheme operated by the trade association to help with disputes.

Electrical Goods: The code is operated by retailers who are members of the Radio, Electrical and Television Retailers' Association (RETRA).
- The retailer's advertisements shall be clear and honest and in accordance with any statutory requirements.
- Goods will be clearly marked with the cash price and, if a discount is offered, it will be explained in precise terms.
- If a deposit is paid, the customer will be advised of a delivery date and if the goods are not delivered on the date specified, a refund or deposit should be offered.
- As much information as possible on how to install and use the product shall be given to the customer.
- New goods are guaranteed by the retailers for parts and labour for a year – this is apart from any manufacturer's guarantee.
- The code covers 'domestic appliances' or 'white goods' like washing machines, spin dryers, refrigerators, toasters and electric cookers and also 'brown goods' which include television sets, radios, stereo equipment and similar items.

Electricity Boards have a similar code which covers servicing and repairs when you purchase 'white goods' from a Board shop and later have them serviced or repaired by the Board.

AMDEA (Association of Manufacturers of Domestic Electrical Appliances) also has a code which operates when you buy a British domestic appliance made by an association member, who then agrees to do the repair work and servicing.

Footwear: This industry has a code prepared by the Footwear Distributors' Federation in consultation with the OFT.
- Shoes should have labels explaining what material the uppers are made of and also giving the country or origin.
- Prices should be inclusive of VAT and customers are entitled to a dated receipt if they ask for one.

■ There is a complaints procedure – the customer can ask for footwear to be sent to a testing centre for an independent report for a very small fee.

Cars: The four main motor trade associations – the Motor Agents' Association, the Society of Motor Manufacturers and Traders, the Vehicle Builders' and Repairers' Association and the Scottish Motor Trade Association – have a voluntary Code of Practice to ensure car buyers get a fair deal.

■ The price quoted in the advertisement must be the same as you pay for a new car. If that price excludes things like delivery charges, number plates or seat belts then that must be clearly shown.

■ If a dealer is required by the manufacturer to carry out a pre-delivery inspection of a new car (and most of them are), he should make available a copy of the type of checklist used.

■ Order forms must show clearly details of **all** charges you will have to pay to put the car on the road.

■ While the car is under guarantee, manufacturing faults can be repaired by any dealer stocking the relevant make, not just the one from whom you bought it.

■ If the car has to be off the road for faults to be corrected, the guarantee period may be extended.

■ If the advertisement quotes the fuel consumption figures, the test methods have to be described. If fuel consumption is compared with other cars, the figures and test methods for the other cars should also be shown.

Second-hand Cars:

■ Any defects must be revealed on an approved checklist which must be prominently displayed and given to the customer before the sale.

■ Where possible a signed statement about the accuracy of a car's mileage should be given.

■ Any price quoted in the advertisement should include VAT.

■ There is a conciliation procedure and an arbitration scheme to help with disputes.

Safety

When we buy goods we don't just want something which looks good and comes in pretty colours. There are other factors the careful shopper takes into consideration before making a choice and safety is one of the most important. There have been many instances where toys, hair curling tongs and even cosmetics have caused harm to those who purchased them and similarly have caused concern to those reponsible for safety legislation.

The Consumer Protection Act 1987 introduced a general duty to trade safely. It is a criminal offence to supply unsafe consumer goods in the United Kingdom. The exceptions are growing crops, water, food, aircraft, motor vehicles, controlled drugs, medicinal products and tobacco.

All the surrounding circumstances are considered such as instructions or warnings given on keeping or consumption of goods, how they are marketed, whether there are existing safety standards and whether the means existed to make goods safer.

In addition there is already a large number of regulations for specific goods detailing safety standards to which they must comply.

Below are some of the goods which are covered by the regulations and which are common household articles. Safety matters concerning labelling are described in Chapter Three and quality control is discussed in Chapter Five.

Aerosols: Regulations set out what sort of propellants may be used and also the volume and other information which must be given on the outside of the container.

Balloons: Any balloon kits which contain benzine are banned from shops.

Carry Cot Stands: These must have passed various strength tests and so be able to hold a cot securely not more than 1.7 inches (4.3 cm) off the floor. The stand should be marked so that the parent knows the maximum size of cot it is designed to hold. There are size limits which vary according to the size of the stand.

Chemicals: Any dangerous substances on sale must be packaged in the kind of container which cannot be corroded by its contents. In addition, the container must have a label which warns the purchaser of any risks involved in using the substances and gives details of any necessary precautions in use.

Cooking Utensils: Anything which comes into contact with food – saucepans, frying pans and so on – is restricted as to the amount of lead which may be used in the metallic coating. Lead can get into food and cause poisoning.

Cosmetics: Any of these products must not contain lead or any substance liable to damage the health of the user.

Crash Helmets: These must be of strong construction and manufactured to set standards.

Electric Blankets: These must be clearly marked to show whether they are over or under blankets and, if the latter, then they must say whether or not they can be used while the bed is occupied. All blankets must carry warnings against misuse and they must be approved by the British Electrotechnical Approvals Board (the only electrical item which must be).

Electrical Equipment: There are general safety standards for most electrical goods which deal with things like adequate insulation. Under these safety regulations, domestic electrical appliances are also required to have safe switches, guards for moving parts, cord grips for leads and live parts not easily accessible. There are specific rules for flexes. Goods must carry a label which explains the colour code for electrical flexes: **blue** for neutral, **brown** for live and **yellow** and **green** for earth.

Fireguards on Heaters: Every sort of heater for domestic use, whether gas, electric or oil must have a fireguard made to the relevant British Standard. The guards must also pass a strength test and an opening test.

Foam-filled Furniture: There have been various attempts to regulate the safety standards of foam-filled furniture, first dealing with the covers and the use of warning labels and since 1 March 1989 all new furniture sold in shops has had to comply with the Furniture and Furnishings (Fire) (Safety) Regulations 1988. These mean firstly that Combination Modified (CM) foam must be used in foam-filled furniture. It is a foam which has been specially formulated to pass the ignitability test in the new regulations. Instead of igniting and spreading as rapidly as ordinary foam it either melts away from a flame or chars.

Secondly, all new furniture available in shops must also have either a covering fabric which resists a specified test with a match flame or a fire-retardant interlining fabric between cover and filling.

Thirdly, the regulations cover the filling of mattresses and bed-bases but not their covers. Shoppers need to look for British Standard 6807 to ensure covers are safe. The regulations also apply to re-upholstery materials, garden furniture suitable for use indoors, new built-in caravan furniture, upholstered headboards, children's furniture and the fillings of cushions and pillows.

Second-hand Furniture: From 1 March 1990 the sale of post-1950 second-hand furniture from shops must comply with previous regulations which specified the covers should resist an ignition test using a smouldering cigarette. Private sales aren't covered.

From 1 March 1993 second-hand furniture for retail sale will have to meet the same safety standards as new furniture. There is an exception which applies to furniture made before 1950 so there will be no restrictions on the sale of period furniture even if it has been reupholstered.

Hood Fastenings on Children's Clothes: No hood on a child's outer garment up to and including age eight or not exceeding 44 cm across the chest when the garment is laid out flat – an anorak, for instance – is allowed to have a drawstring fastening, in case the child strangles.

Medicines: Pills and tablets of aspirin and paracetamol must be packed in sealed units (a foil pack for instance with the individual tablets sealed in) or in a childproof container. However, the chemist must give an adult customer a non-childproof pack of pills if the customer requests it.

Night-dresses: Those for children must be made of flame-resistant material which conforms to the relevant British Standard. Night-dresses for adults must either be flame resistant or carry a warning to the effect that they should be kept away from fire. And if a night-dress has been given some sort of chemical treatment to make it safe then it must carry a label which warns the buyer not to boil it or bleach it because this could harm the properties of the fabric.

These regulations apply only to night-dresses and not to pyjamas, dressing gowns or baby gowns, although the Home Office recommends that the two latter types of garment should also be flame resistant.

Oil Heaters: These must pass a stability test and be fitted with an automatic cut out so that, if the heater is overturned while lit, the flame automatically goes out within 15 seconds. There should be a secure way of fixing the heater so that it doesn't fall but, if it does, then only a small quantity of fuel should spill out. Heaters must not give off smoke or excessive carbon monoxide or have an unguarded flame. The outside of the heater, the guard and the unused fuel must not get too hot.

Pencils: The paint or varnish on pencils and the writing elements of pencils, crayons and chalks must not contain more than specified amounts of lead for fear of harming anyone who licks or sucks pencils.

Toys: These must be flame resistant and must not be covered in any poisonous paint, lacquer or varnish. They should not have any sharp edges or spikes and there should be no possibility of children swallowing glass eyes from the faces of toys. Any mains-operated items must conform to electrical safety rules and there should be no danger of a child suffocating from plastic bags in which toys may be packed.

How Can You Tell Whether A Product Is Safe Or Not?

You should look out for certain symbols which signify safety in the product.

This is the **British Standards Safety Mark** and it is to be seen only on those goods which comply with the standards for safety set down by the British Standards Institution. It is found mostly on gas appliances such as fires, cookers and on some electric light fittings.

Look for this **BEAB** label if you are shopping for any electrical gadget. If a product has this label it means that it has been passed as safe by the **British Electrotechnical Approvals Board**. Many household articles, for example, food mixers, kettles, toasters and other pieces of electrical equipment carry it. But remember that it is voluntary! It is entirely up to individual firms to decide whether or not to put their products to the board for approval. The only item which must, by law, have BEAB approval, is an electric blanket.

Electrical equipment with this sign on the rating plate or body of the appliance indicates double insulation which does not require an earth wire. Found on television sets, electric lawnmowers, hair dryers, electric drills and vacuum cleaners, amongst other items.

The **Corgi** symbol is more an indication of a firm's competence in terms of safety rather than that of a product. The letters stand for **Confederation for the Registration of Gas Installers** and mean that a firm has gained the necessary approval to carry out work on gas installations complying with British Standard Codes of Practice and Government safety regulations.

Another safety safeguard: this time it's the sign of the **National Inspection Council for Electrical Installation Contracting** which gives protection against unsafe or faulty workmanship. An electrical contractor who displays this sign has agreed to have work checked periodically by an NICEIC engineer, to ensure that it complies with current regulations. You can therefore be assured of good workmanship and a safe installation or recourse to the Council if there are any problems.

What Can You Do If You Buy A Product Which Is Not Safe?

■ Report it to your local Trading Standards or Consumer Protection Office. Under the Consumer Protection Act 1987 it is a criminal offence to supply unsafe consumer goods in the United Kingdom.

A Trading Standards Officer is authorised to issue suspension notices to retailers prohibiting the sale of goods which are unsafe, and if necessary the officer can also apply to the magistrates court for an order for the goods to be destroyed.

■ Go back to the shop where you bought the article and ask for your money back. If the item turns out to be dangerous, then the shop can hardly claim it was fit for its purpose in the first place! So, under the Sale of Goods Act, you'd be entitled to a refund of your money.

Product Liability

The Consumer Protection Act 1987 introduced new rights for consumers injured by defective products.

In the past those injured had to prove a manufacturer negligent before they could successfully sue for damages. The Act removes the need to prove negligence. A buyer can already sue a supplier without proof of negligence under the Sale of Goods Act. Now anyone injured by a defective product has the right to sue the producer, importer or own-brand supplier.

A person can sue under the Act for compensation for

■ death
■ injury
■ private property valued above £275

Quality

We can get some protection against poor quality if we look for goods which carry the 'Kitemark'.

This symbol tells the customer that the product has been manufactured to the standard set down by the British

Standards Institution. That in turn guarantees that it has been thoroughly tested for performance and should, therefore, have the sort of durability which most budget-conscious shoppers look for. There are over 3,000 British Standards drawn up for household appliances alone, plus others for many other products as diverse as school blazers and glass for doors.

There are standards for motor-cycle helmets, prams, electric showers for the bathroom and even hot water bottles.

The thing to remember is that it is a purely voluntary scheme and manufacturers have a choice as to whether they put their products forward for testing or not. The wise shopper, however, faced with two similar products will choose the one with the Kitemark.

Advertising

The consumer gets certain protection as a result of the British Code of Advertising Practice which is operated by the Advertising Standards Authority (ASA). Although the code has no force of law, any member of the public who feels an advertisement goes against the terms of the code should send details of their complaint to the ASA who will investigate it and publish their findings in their quarterly reports. The code gives the following protection concerning product advertising.

- Products should not be described as 'free' where there is any cost to the consumer other than the actual cost of any delivery, freight or postage.
- Advertisements about hair and scalp products shouldn't claim that baldness can be prevented or retarded, that thinning of the hair can be arrested, that hair growth can be stimulated or that hair itself can be strengthened.
- Slimming claims are not acceptable for massage or vibrator machines, inflatable garments, sauna baths or bath essences.
- In the case of commemorative items and others produced in limited editions, the number of articles to be produced in any limited edition should be stated in all promotional material. Claims about the investment potential of the articles on sale should make it clear that there can be no guarantee of any future increase in value.
- Research results should not be misused, nor should quotations from technical and scientific literature in support of a product.
- Claims for prices or performance, which use formulas such as 'up to x miles per gallon' or 'prices from as low as £x' are not acceptable where there is any chance of the consumer being misled about the availability of the benefits offered.

Guarantees

Most manufacturers accept the fact that no production line is perfect and that even the most stringent quality control can't stop the odd defect going unnoticed. That defect may show up sooner or later as far as the purchaser of the product is concerned.

Obviously if a hair curler doesn't work from the moment you plug it in or if it stops curling when you've only used it twice, then the correct course of action is to take it back to the retailer and claim a refund. But what so often happens in practice is that the product only shows signs of being defective many months after you've bought it, and that can make claiming one's rights under the Sale of Goods Act a little more open to argument (at least as far as the retailer is concerned!). The manufacturer's guarantee comes in very handy indeed in such a situation.

What Exactly is a Guarantee?

The manufacturer's guarantee is a written promise that he will put right any defects in either parts or workmanship free of charge or at very little cost, alway providing that it occurs within a certain period of time from the purchase date. Normally a guarantee covers a year, but in the case of some colour televisions, for instance, it can be two years and with something like sunglasses it might only be six months.

Comparatively new is a five-year guarantee on some larger household items – but this isn't completely free of charge. It is in fact an 'extension' guarantee over and above the initial year's free guarantee and you get the extra time for a one-off payment which can vary from £12 to £20 depending on the value of the item.

Incidentally, there is no legal obligation on the part of any manufacturer to provide a guarantee but these days most do if they make electrical and mechanical goods of some sort.

Once a guarantee is given, the manufacturer is bound to stick by the terms of it. But those terms decide what the firm's actual obligations are towards the purchaser, so it's well worth reading the guarantee before you put it away in a safe place. When the fridge stops working or the iron's thermostat fails it's far too late for you to find out that you aren't as well covered as you'd thought!

Legal Restrictions on the Terms

A guarantee must not attempt to exclude one's normal rights against the seller (under the Sale of Goods Act) or to restrict the liability of the manufacturer himself for damage or negligence. Since November 1978 a guarantee must, in fact, positively state that it does not in any way affect the customer's statutory rights. Any guarantee which does not contain such a statement could mean the firm risks prosecution under the Fair Trading Act. So, if you come across one, then report it to your local Trading Standards or Consumer Protection Office.

Labour Charges

These are sometimes not covered with the result that the firm will only supply the actual part free of charge not the labour required to fit it.

Carriage

This may well be an extra cost to the customer and covers the cost of parts being transported from factory to service agent. If it's a small item such as a hair dryer you may have to pack it up and send it off yourself to the firm for 'free' repair under the guarantee. Of course, the postage and packing are not 'free'; you have to pay for them.

Components

These days many parts of the same product are made by different firms and simply bought in on a sub-contract basis by the main manufacturer. And this is one area where the customer can very easily be caught out in the guarantee. Often the main manufacturer disclaims all responsibility for components not manufactured by him and unfortunately in these circumstances the customer has absolutely no way of telling in advance which parts were supplied by the manufacturer and which were not!

Country

Guarantees may state that they are only valid in certain countries. Some operate only in England, Scotland and Wales and exclude Northern Ireland or the Channel Islands. Other multi-national firms may give guarantees which are valid worldwide and indeed they give a list of service agents as far apart as Zanzibar and America.

Compensation

This is not usually offered and so it's unlikely that you could make a claim for compensation from the manufacturer under a guarantee if, for instance, you were planning a special evening out and your hair curling tongs wouldn't work.

The Guarantee Card

Some cards do say quite specifically that unless you fill in the card and send it off within seven days, then you have no rights under the guarantee. Since the firm has no legal obligation to give a guarantee in the first place, it is quite entitled to make this condition! Most reputable companies will not refuse to help even if you forget to send the card providing you can produce some sort of proof of purchase. But don't take any chances, send the card off anyway – you've nothing to lose. Some of the 'extra time' guarantees for a single payment do say that unless you send off the payment within a certain time from the purchase date you lose the opportunity to take advantage of the extra offer. So watch out for that.

Retailers' Guarantees

Several shops in the radio, television and electrical business these days (particularly if they are members of RETRA) offer their own 12-month guarantees for parts and labour in addition to the manufacturer's guarantee. In this case you have the choice of taking the item back to the shop if a fault shows up during the first year, rather than going to the manufacturer – and that can get you quicker service. The retailer's guarantee is often simply written on to the front of your invoice or, alternatively, is set out on the back of your receipt with all the conditions clearly detailed. In either case you must remember to hang on to the receipt!

Insurance

The products we purchase can develop defects or stop working or become dangerous and, as we've seen, there are certain steps we can take to remedy matters. But our possessions might also be damaged by fire, by water rushing out from burst pipes in the attic, or they might be stolen when someone breaks into our home.

In such an event the seller of the fridge, the television set or the furniture is not going to help us, nor are we going to get any kind of redress from the manufacturer. But an insurance policy will help.

An average home contains something like £20,000 worth of goods bought over the years and so it is very important that we protect them. A contents insurance policy will cover everything in the house from the cooker and the tumble dryer to carpets, furniture, television set, tape recorder, pictures and include soft furnishing, hair dryers, cutlery, glasses and even the gardening tools.

There are two kinds of contents policy available – 'indemnity' and 'replacement as new'. If you insure on an 'indemnity' basis you will be paid the cost of repairing damaged articles or of replacing what's stolen or destroyed **less** an amount for wear and tear depending on the age of the item. On a 'replacement as new' basis, you will be paid the full cost of repairs if the item is damaged or the cost of replacing the **equivalent new** articles if stolen or destroyed.

What you have to do is go from room to room, not leaving out the garage or the garden shed, and note down everything. Work out what it would cost to replace them at today's prices. If you are working on an 'indemnity' basis then an allowance for wear and tear should be deducted. Television sets, for instance, are calculated to last for about ten years, so for every year you have owned your set, deduct one tenth of the price of a new one. For a 'new for old' policy simply put down the replacement cost (at today's prices) of all items.

Stolen Goods

If you buy something which seemed like a bargain at the time, but later turns out to be stolen – what's your position?

Generally speaking, the person who buys goods from someone who does not own them and has no right to sell, will lose out. The goods must be returned to their original owner.

There are, however, a few exceptions where one is allowed to retain the goods even if they were stolen.

■ If the sale takes place in an open, public and legally constituted market. This is known as 'market overt' and applies to the recognised markets in any of England's market towns. In London the term applies to shops within the ancient City of London (but **only** to shops within that boundary).

■ **NOTE:** In Scotland and Wales there is no 'market overt' and so this particular protection regarding stolen goods is not available to the consumer.

■ If you buy goods from someone who has paid for them with a dud cheque they are yours providing you buy them before the original owner cancels the deal.

■ If you buy a motor car or motor bike in good faith and without knowing of any outstanding HP but the original owner has not paid off the hire purchase instalments, you can keep it. Note that this rule only applies to cars and motor bikes – in the case of other goods, the finance company can take back goods.

The best way to protect yourself against buying stolen goods is always to be very wary of what appear to be perfect or near perfect goods offered to you at an unbelievably low price!

SIX

COMPLAINTS

We buy so many different products every day that something is almost bound to go wrong with some of them. Surveys show that as many as one in ten purchases can turn out to be faulty. Perhaps the new washing machine spills water all over the kitchen floor, the heel falls off a shoe at the very first wearing or the bag of flour from the supermarket has small creatures living in it!

When that sort of thing happens we get angry, we feel very frustrated and we tell our friends and neighbours exactly what we think of that particular product or supplier. And, having let off steam, we may even make a complaint to the proper place! The fact that so many complaints land on the desks of consumer organizations, Citizens Advice Bureaux and the Office of Fair Trading every year is evidence of the fact that some of those who buy faulty goods do complain.

Unfortunately, just as many complaints are not recorded because consumers don't know where to complain, how to complain or even if it is worth complaining at all! And that's a pity, because it leaves so many firms saying rather smugly, 'Oh we don't get many complaints, madam, I'm sure you must have misused our product!' to the brave person who dares to ring up or write a letter questioning the quality of their goods. The truth is that many have found a product wanting but have simply suffered in silence.

Complaints procedures may indeed be inadequate and lack the potential for remedy or redress of the methods used by continental countries. But it is still better to complain every time we have real cause because every time we do, it's one step towards improving things for ourselves and our fellow consumers. We must argue our case from a position of strength and we can only do that if we know exactly what our rights are in any given situation.

When we buy goods of any kind, we are entering into a contract with the seller. We offer to buy and pay money and, in accepting that offer, the seller has certain obligations under the contract: the goods must be of **'merchantable quality'** which means that goods must be reasonably fit for their normal purpose bearing in mind the price paid, the nature of the goods and how they were described. So, if you buy an electric drill and discover that it won't drill when you plug it in, you would have cause for complaint. But there are, in fact, two exceptions to this 'merchantable quality' provision that many customers are either not aware of or just prefer to forget about! These are:

■ If the shop points out certain defects in the product and the customer still agrees to buy, he cannot then go back at a later date and claim the goods are not of 'merchantable quality' because of the defect drawn to his attention.

■ If the buyer examines the goods before agreeing to buy them and does not spot defects which would normally be obvious to anyone – in other words if you were to try on a jacket which had no buttons on it, bought it and then took it back to the shop claiming it to be defective because of its lack of buttons – you would not have a case!

The goods should be **'fit for any particular purpose for which they are being bought'**. If a customer goes into a shop and asks the assistant for a cleaner which will cope with a particular task, then the cleaner offered should do the job. The shop is expected to have some sort of knowledge and expertise of the goods they sell – something many a customer might well dispute! It may seem unfair on a shop, but one must remember that they always have the option of telling a customer that they simply don't know which product would be suitable and that leaves the customer to decide whether to make his or her own choice or go to a shop where the assistants are more knowledgeable.

The goods must be **'as described'** and that means described either on the package or by the shop selling them. Quite simply, if a pair of shoes have 'made from real leather' stamped on them, then they should not turn out to be made of plastic; and, if a set of towels is described as blue on the box, then they must not be pink because 'blue' is part of your contract with the shopkeeper.

These obligations are set down under the Sale of Goods Act 1979. They apply to all goods you buy from shops (whether or not in a sale), from street traders, by mail order and from door-to-door salesmen and cover every type of product from food to furniture. But these obligations **do not** apply when you buy something from a private individual as opposed to 'in the course of business' from a shopkeeper with the one exception that goods must be as described. So if a private seller describes an item as 'being made of suede' or 'five years old' or whatever, and this is later proved to be not true, you can sue him.

Since this is a private seller's only obligation, buying from a private source needs extra care and attention. Equally, if you offer goods for sale privately, you must be careful only to make claims which are true.

Second-hand Goods

When a trader sells something second-hand it will probably not be in perfect condition, but it is still covered by the Sale of Goods Act. A second-hand cooker may have lost some of its sparkle, but it should be of merchantable quality and fit for its purpose – capable of cooking meals.

Its condition is judged by many factors including the price paid, the age of the article and how it was described.

In the case of a second-hand car bought from a trader you would certainly be able to reject it if it were in a dangerous condition when sold.

Remember, too, that no one can take the customer's rights under the Sale of Goods Act away from him by displaying a notice or inserting clauses in order forms or whatever. Any such clause or notice is completely without force.

Rights of Redress

If something goes wrong with the goods we buy, we have two basic rights we can claim under the law:

■ A full refund of the money we have paid when we return the goods and cancel the contract. If, however, the defect is very minor or the purchaser does not report the defect quickly, then he may only be entitled to an amount of money which will compensate for the reduced value of the goods, or a repair may be agreed in such a case.

■ Damages to compensate for the fault and any loss it may have caused. The object of this is to put the purchaser into the same position as he would have been in had the contract been fulfilled. So you would be entitled to the cost of a repair if you had it carried out by someone other than the seller and also compensation for any damage caused as a result of the fault – for instance, if a faulty washing machine had torn your clothes.

In practice you may be perfectly happy to have the item exchanged for another which **does** work. Alternatively, you may be satisfied with a repair to the original product. But these remedies are a matter to be agreed between customer and retailer – the only actual legal entitlement is money.

Be careful that by accepting a repair you don't lose your right to reject should the repair prove to be unsatisfactory. It can sometimes be the case that there is some inherent defect in a piece of equipment, which can be corrected on a 'temporary' basis by a repair but which will recur in a few days or a few weeks. So, if you do accept a repair, send a letter to the retailer to protect your rights to a refund, such as:

> On . . . (date) I bought a toaster from your shop which, after using only once, has proved to be faulty. The defective element is your responsibility and so I am rejecting the toaster.
>
> However, without prejudice to my rights, I would consider having a repair to the element, providing it can be done quickly and efficiently. If not, I shall rely on my right of rejection under the Sale of Goods Act and will want a refund of the money I paid for the toaster.

Shops will very often offer a customer a credit note when faced with faulty goods. **Be very wary of this.** You are under no obligation to accept the note and, if there's nothing else suitable in the shop, you could find it very difficult to get your money back. Even worse, you'll have handed back the original goods and have lost your evidence that they are faulty.

QUESTIONS TO ASK

When do I lose my right to reject goods?

The difference between being able to reject goods because they are not 'merchantable', not 'fit for a particular purpose', or not 'as described' and only being able to claim damages instead is very important to the buyer. The right to reject is effectively lost when the buyer has 'accepted' the goods.

The Sale of Goods Act describes acceptance as taking place when:
- the buyer intimates to the seller that s/he has accepted them
- the buyer does something in relation to the goods which is inconsistent with the seller's ownership
- a reasonable time passes and the buyer retains the goods without rejecting them.

The first point is most straightforward, although lawyers argue over whether traders who ask buyers to sign 'acceptance notes' after delivery can rely on them for this point.

The second point would cover instances where the buyer sold the goods, customised them or incorporated them into something else.

For the third point, what is a reasonable time? The judge in the case of Bernstein v. Pampsons Motors said that it was not a reasonable time to discover a particular defect; it meant a reasonable time to inspect the goods and try them out generally. The length of time would vary for different goods. He found that Mr Bernstein, who had only had his new car for three weeks before it broke down and he rejected it, had had a reasonable time to try the car out generally: in three weeks he had made two or three short trips for this very purpose. He was awarded damages instead of a refund.

In a different case involving a motor car, five months elapsed before it was rejected because the seriousness and potential danger of the faults reported to the seller took some time to establish. The judge decided the buyer could reject.

The Office of Fair Trading advises consumers that they can reject goods as defective only when they have hardly used the goods and have acted at once.

Is there a time limit on complaining?

Bearing in mind that you may not be able to reject goods once a reasonable time has elapsed, your claim for damages can be made theoretically at any time up to six years after the purchase. You will always have to prove that what has gone wrong is due to the condition the goods were in when they were bought. In other words, merchantable quality applies to the time the goods are supplied.

You can see it becomes more difficult to show this the longer you have goods and the more they are used. The shop may argue that a fault is due to wear and tear or misuse. If this is the case you will need to get evidence from a completely independent source and this will cost you money.

So you can claim a full refund if you reject the goods, and damages once you have 'accepted' them. Your claim for damages is normally the difference between the purchase price and the value of the goods in their faulty condition or the cost of putting the fault right. Sometimes retailers offer partial refunds. Extra compensation can be claimed if the faulty goods cause damage.

Some trade associations do have a test facility for which they charge a fee, but in the main it's up to the customer to provide his own evidence. So until all goods come with a little label attached to them proclaiming their 'minimum durability' spelled out in months or years, the general rule is 'reject as quickly as possible after purchase' or you may find yourself in a dispute with the retailer and have no choice but to accept a repair, or claim damages.

Some Other Points

The Trade Descriptions Act makes it a criminal offence for a trader to describe goods falsely either in print, by word of mouth or by illustration. And that rule covers almost every sort of description – size, quantity, strength, performance, material and so on. Take your complaint to your local Trading Standards or Consumer Protection Department.

Credit Companies

When you buy something on credit, quite often the finance arrangements come not from the shop but from a quite separate source, such as a bank or a finance house. This can, in fact, provide a double protection to the customer in the case of a later complaint about faulty goods.

Under the Consumer Credit Act, it may be that whoever provides you with the credit facilities has an equal responsibility with the seller of the goods, should these goods prove faulty. Some examples of dual responsibility would be a) where the supplier of the goods puts the customer in touch with a firm which will supply credit to finance the purchase; b) where there is a trading check arrangement; or c) where a credit card is used to pay for goods or services. This applies to credit agreements where the cash price is more than £100 and less than £30,000, and the credit is less than £15,000.

■ **NOTE:** It is important to bear in mind that equal liability does not apply where you arrange a personal loan, which you spend as you wish and which is not tied to paying for a specific item named in the agreement.

It's usually better to go to the seller first if goods are faulty but you can also claim against the firm supplying the credit if the first course of action fails.

Hire Purchase, Conditional Sale, Credit Sale

In these agreements the Finance Company is also the legal supplier of the goods. So any claims for faulty goods would have to be made against the Finance Company alone although its often sensible to try to sort it out with the shop first. There are no cash limits for claims under these agreements.

Complaints about Faulty Goods

When we know exactly what our rights are and are able, if necessary, to quote the relevant law to the retailer, we can set about exercising those rights. None of us enjoys making a fuss, but none of us enjoys wasting money either and we are entitled to get products that do the job they're supposed to do.

Firstly, go back to the retailer from whom you bought the goods. If the product is small then take it back with you but, if it's too large to carry, then take instead all the relevant bits of paper such as receipts. This is why it's extremely important to hang on to the receipts you get for purchases – because unless you have a cheque stub or can take a witness to prove you did buy the item at that shop, your receipt may be the only evidence of purchase.

Incidentally, **never** hand over receipts or other documents when you are making a complaint. The best thing to do is to pop along to your local library or railway station and use the copying machine there and then take the copy along when you complain.

Secondly, ask to speak to the manager, the supervisor or buyer – if it's a large department store – or the owner, if it's a small business. State your complaint and give precise details of what's gone wrong.

Thirdly, if he agrees that you have a justifiable complaint, then tell him what action you would like the shop to take. Bear in mind that your only **legal** entitlement is a refund of your money and/or damages but, if you'd rather have a replacement, for instance, or would be happy to accept a free repair, then state your preference. Don't accept a credit note offered unless you are sure that's what you want. In shops which have a reputation for handling customers' complaints promptly, you will no doubt find the situation resolved satisfactorily at this point. However, if the shop refuses to give you a refund of your money or even to acknowledge their obligation or that the article is faulty, suggest the manager looks up the Sale of Goods Act in his local library and leave the shop quietly.

If you have had no satisfaction from the previous stages, when you get back home, sit down and write a letter to the managing director of the firm, shop or organization. If, for instance, it's one of a chain, write to the managing director at the Head Office (details are often to be found on receipts).

Keep the letter brief and to the point. Simply state the shop where you bought the item, the date, the type of goods and the cost. Give details of the exact model number of the article and also the date and number of the receipt. Explain what went wrong and what action you have already taken to get things put right. Finish off by telling him whether you want a refund or a replacement and **do** quote your rights under the Sales of Goods Act. Ask for an early reply.

Although it will cost a little more, consider sending the letter by recorded delivery to be sure that it does get attention, when it arrives.

If you know that the firm has a Customer Relations Department you could address the letter there, but in practice many firms, particularly the smaller ones, deal with complaints through the managing director's office – which usually means his secretary!

This should have the desired effect, but if you get no response to your letter, then write once more and on the second occasion it is worth mentioning that you intend to send a copy to a particular consumer programme or a consumer column in a newspaper or magazine. Few firms welcome the prospect of bad publicity. Working in the media, I know from first-hand experience just how effective it can be in helping customers resolve complaints against firms.

If you follow all these steps and still get nowhere, what do you do? There are several alternatives. You could go along to a local Citizens Advice Bureau, Consumer Advice Centre or Legal Advice Centre taking all the details of your complaint with you. If the expert staff there feel you have a good case they may take it up with the retailer on your behalf and may well be more successful.

Alternatively, you could contact the relevant trade association if the retailer is a member. Many have a conciliation scheme for consumer complaints and even some form of arbitration. (Details of these associations are given in Chapter Two). You could ask a radio or television consumer programme or a consumer journalist to take up the matter of your behalf. They have a high success rate, but they usually get so many requests for help that they can only take on a limited number.

The manufacturer is another possibility. He has **no responsibility** in the matter of faulty goods unless injury or damage has been caused (see Product Liability page 65), but most manufacturers are rather jealous of their reputations and the quality of their products. So it does no harm at all, if you've had no luck with the seller of the goods, to drop a brief note to the manufacturer (address usually to be found on the packaging of the product) explaining the problems resulting from the faulty goods, the retailer's refusal to take any action and that you are not overly impressed by the quality of the goods! You may get a better response with this approach.

If a faulty product carries a Kitemark (see page 65), the another option you could try is to get in touch with the British Standards Institution's Quality Assurance Department (Chapter Two) giving them the details and they might just take it up with the manufacturer concerned.

Politeness! As you progress through various complaint procedures it's most important never to lose your temper. However much you may feel like being abusive – don't be – it invariably makes matters worse! A 'good complainer' needs patience, persistence, politeness and knowledge of his rights. And if that doesn't bring results then the only option left is to take your case to court.

Deliveries

When a customer orders goods which are not in stock he is quite entitled to specify a date when he requires the goods and this then becomes part of the contract with the supplier. Always get a delivery date in writing so that there can be no dispute later (ask the sales assistant to write it on both his and your copy of the order).

If the goods don't turn up by the date given – and, unfortunately, surveys show that very often major items arrive many weeks late – the supplier has, in effect, broken the contract. So the customer has the right to say, 'You didn't deliver at the agreed time – I no longer want the suite of furniture and I'll go elsewhere.' If a deposit has been paid, which is normal, then that deposit must be returned when you cancel because of non-delivery.

However, if you've been naive and have not spelled out a date for delivery, all is not yet lost! The supplier still has a duty to deliver within a 'reasonable' time, say a month in the case of a fairly major purchase. So, if the article hasn't turned up in a reasonable time, go back to the shop, tell them quietly but firmly that you can't wait for much longer and that you will give them another 14 days and, if the goods still haven't arrived, you'll cancel the order and want your money back. Give that ultimatum in writing. But be careful: once you have agreed to wait that extra 14 days, three weeks or whatever, you can't cancel and demand your money back during that time.

So, to avoid problems, always insist on a delivery date being agreed with the supplier and written down. It's amazing how often sales assistants will assure customers that an article will be 'here in a week without fail' and a month later you're still sitting on the floor waiting for the armchair!

Exchange of Goods of the Wrong Size or Colour

Many shops are, in fact, willing to exchange goods for such a reason. This may be an admirable scheme, but it does tend to confuse customers about their basic rights! Many shoppers expect this 'exchange facility' from all shops when they see it offered in a few, and can even be convinced that they have a legal entitlement to it. **This is not so** – it's a gesture of goodwill on the part of that particular shop.

So what do you do if you buy an article and you're not sure whether it will fit or suit the person for whom you're buying it? The trick here is to ask the sales assistant before you buy if you can bring the article back and exchange it for another size or colour if it isn't suitable. If she agrees, then the 'exchange facility' becomes an integral part of your contract with the shop, which means that they are bound to honour their promise to exchange, if that should be necessary. **Always** get such an arrangement written on your receipt, so that there can be no dispute later. Otherwise, by the time you take the article back the sales assistant who agreed to the exchange might have been moved to another counter or be on holiday and you will have absolutely no proof that such an arrangement was ever made. If necessary, write on the receipt yourself and get the assistant to 'OK' it by adding her initials.

If You Can't Find Anyone to Complain to

Some businesses go bust, others simply seem to disappear and the customer can be left without goods they've paid for or perhaps with only some of them. You'll certainly feel like complaining, but the problem may be to actually find someone to complain to if you are faced with empty premises and a notice on the door saying 'Business Closed'.

Try the local rates department. They are not under any obligation at all to give details about the business, but if you make a personal visit and explain exactly why you want the information you may be lucky.

Check with your local police station in case they have any information and also with the Trading Standards Department (they may have had other complaints about the firm).

If it is not a limited company but a partnership or a one-man business, then the partners or the owner are completely liable for any debts. If you do trace the owners and they refuse to refund your money or give you the goods, you can sue them. Once upon a time traders (except those trading under their own name) had to register with a Business Registry and in that had to state their full name and address. This meant that any member of the public had access to that information in Registration Offices in England, Scotland and Wales. Unhappily, that legislation was repealed in 1982 and one cannot now check in this way. However, after the law was repealed, the London Chamber of Commerce started a voluntary Register of Business Names. The information is available to members of the public – all they have to do is contact the office of the Chamber of Commerce who run the Registry.

Limited Companies

In a limited company, the individual directors have, as the name indicates, a 'limited' liability for company debts. This is good for business, but bad for customers if trading difficulties arise.

■ If a receiver is appointed, write to him giving details of any money owed and register your claim against the company. Under a receiver, the company doesn't actually stop trading but he takes over the running of it and generally stops payment to those owed money (creditors). However, he may put the company on its feet again and claims will eventually be met. If the company is told to pay debts, certain things have preference (taxes and wages, for instance) and money owed to customers usually comes last on the list.

■ **Liquidation** means that the company stops trading. The liquidator collects all the money owing to the company, sells all the assets and then distributes any money to creditors. The big drawback is that generally there is not sufficient money to pay everyone in full and there is a 'pay-out' order the liquidator is bound to follow and 'unsecured creditors' – which is simply the technical jargon for members of the public owed money – come almost last on the list yet again. So usually they end up with nothing at all, or at the very most, a small percentage of what they should get – for instance, 10 pence for every pound owed to them.

Thus, in the case of either a receivership or liquidation, register your claim immediately, by writing to the company with the details and obviously enclosing copies of all receipts and order forms which you have. If a firm goes into liquidation or receivership then, generally, a meeting of all creditors will be arranged, usually advertised in local papers, so you can go along to find out exactly what the position is.

Avoiding Action

There are ways in which the wise customer can reduce the risk of losing out through a business folding up, disappearing without trace or going into liquidation. Here is a checklist.

■ Just as many firms require a bank reference before lending money to customers, so a customer is similarly quite entitled to get a bank reference for any firm they are about to trust with their money. To do this you need to ask the company for the name and address of their bank. Give that information to your own bank and ask the manager to do the necessary check with the company's bank. When he gets their reply, ask him to 'interpret' it for you, as often the wording is not as clear as it might be.

■ **WARNING:** If the company refuses to give you the name and address of their bank, then think very carefully before proceeding with your order. Just remember that if **you** refused to give a bank reference to a company they'd probably refuse to deal with you. Reputable companies are normally happy to supply information about their banks, if asked.

■ Limited companies, in return for limited liability, must register with Companies House and file annual accounts. Copies of information on limited companies can be obtained by post on payment of a few pounds from the address in Chapter Two.

■ Try, if possible, to pick a firm which has been recommended to you by someone, and has proved satisfactory. If it's a local firm, ask around and try to discover how long it has been established and what is performance has been in the past.

■ Perhaps the golden rule is don't pay in advance. On the other hand, sometimes people do order things and then simply deny that they did so, which can leave a shop with, for instance, a piece of carpet cut precisely to fit your room and useless to anyone else – so the fairest system all round is for the customer to pay a deposit in advance (say 10% of the purchase price).

■ If anyone has doubts about a company's financial reliability, then perhaps the simplest sort of self-protection is to use credit. If you buy on credit, the firm which lends you the money (normally separate from the supplier) may have a liability in terms of missing or faulty goods – so contact it. This also applies when you buy goods using a credit card.

Prompt Action

If you should have the misfortune to deal with a company which goes out of business then always take immediate action to try to recoup your losses. And to prevent others making the same mistake it's as well to alert your local Trading Standards Office.

SEVEN

SERVICES

What is a Service?

Every time we ask someone to do something for us we are requesting a service, because the word means any work performed by one person for another. In consumer terms, the range of services we use – and pay for – is quite enormous. When we switch on the electric fire or send a parcel, we are taking advantage of one of the 'nationalized' services.

In the private sector, an even greater diversity of services is on offer. We need to have our car repaired from time to time and when the washing machine floods, the television screen goes blank or the video stops recording we call in an expert to put it right. The repair we require may be major – perhaps the roof requires replacing or the chimney stack rebuilding. Or we may be seeking an improvement, whether it's the addition of a whole new room to the house or just double glazing installed for the winter.

In the High Street there are dry cleaners, hairdressers, furniture removers, estate agents, insurance companies, accountants and surveyors – all of them providing us with a service.

We visit the doctors, dentists and opticians and to reach any of them we may well have to make use of another service – transport.

We all use more or less of the different services according to our circumstance and our personal tastes and habits. But a large number of us are totally dissatisfied with them.

Services and Our Rights

These are not so clearly set out in law as those which apply when we buy goods (Sale of Goods Act), see Chapter Six. Our rights when buying services were to be found in the law of contract and common law cases. However, one single act to cover them – the Supply of Goods and Services Act 1982 – has been in force from early 1983.

It should make things easier for consumers in England, Wales and Northern Ireland, at least. Scotland, originally included in the bill, was removed from it at the third reading. It's important to note, though, that the bill **does not** provide even the English, Welsh, or Irish with any new rights: it simply sets out the existing ones in a single piece of legislation. So the Scots still have exactly the same rights as the rest of the UK – but have to look harder for them!

Our Basic Rights

■ **Quality and Performance:** The customer is entitled to expect the supplier of services to carry out the work with reasonable skill and care. And when materials are supplied as part of the contract then they must be 'as described', 'of merchantable quality' and 'fit for their purpose'.

■ **Loss or Damage:** If you suffer loss or damage as a result of work not being properly done you should be able to claim compensation from the firm.

■ **Delays:** Suppliers of any type of service do have a legal duty to carry out the work within a reasonable time. However, it is a court's interpretation of what is reasonable which is the deciding factor in any case. If, on the other hand, a time for completion of the work was stipulated in writing at the outset, then one could hold the firm to that date or take appropriate action if they did not keep to it. And if a time is advertised – for instance 'same day delivery' or 'cleaned in 24 hours' and that claim is not fulfilled, the trader can be prosecuted under the Trade Descriptions Act which applies to services just as it does to goods.

■ **Payment:** If a customer does not agree a price in advance, then he is obliged only to pay a 'reasonable price'. Determining 'reasonable' can, of course, be tricky. The best plan is to ask at least two other firms locally to give you a quotation for the same job, send copies to the firm you feel is making an exorbitant charge and send a sum of money which is average, based on the quotations you get. The best way to avoid any dispute about a price for a job is, of course, to establish the cost in advance, either by an estimate or a quotation.

An estimate is simply an indication – a rough guess – of what the cost is likely to be. As such, it isn't binding. In the event the firm can charge you very much more for the job and you might be hard put to complain.

A quotation, on the other hand, is a firm price which, if accepted by the customer, is legally binding on the contractor. In other words he can't charge more. Always make sure a quotation is actually marked with the word 'Quotation' otherwise the firm may charge you more and argue that they gave you an estimate!

■ **Exclusion Clauses: Liability for Negligence** The Unfair Contract Terms Act (1977) protected consumers against firms providing services who attempted to escape their liability for death or injury due to negligence by using exclusion clauses in their terms of business.

This firm accepts no liability for any injury caused to any person whether or not as a result of negligence on the part of any member of the firm's staff.

That kind of condition is no longer valid and anyone suffering injury is still able to sue for damages through the courts.

In terms of loss or damage the position unfortunately, is less clear. Any exclusion clause can only be upheld if it is considered 'reasonable'. But to establish whether or not it is reasonable a customer would have to take the case to court and accept the court's interpretation of the word. In some instances companies have not insisted on sticking to these clauses when it has been pointed out to them that they may well be against the terms of the Unfair Contract Terms Act they have simply paid up. And in other cases which did go to court, clauses limiting a company's liability have been held to be 'unreasonable'. However, none of these has really set legal precedents and it is still very much a matter of each individual case being decided on its own merits.

■ **Liability for Contracts** Where a trader contracts with a consumer there are three ways that liability cannot be excluded *unless reasonable*:

☐ liability for breach of contract

☐ the trader cannot deviate from the contract

☐ the trader cannot refuse to perform part or all of the contract

So if the trader tries to rely on an exclusion clause to stop you making a complaint or claiming compensation, point out that s/he will have to prove the clause is reasonable.

If you think any clause in a contract limiting liability is unreasonable and you have suffered loss or damage, then go to a Citizens Advice Bureau or Consumer Advice Centre for guidance in pursuing your claim through the courts.

Codes of Practice

Besides these basic rights under the law, very many of those in the service industries belong to a trade association and work to Codes of Practice. The codes are generally agreed with the Office of Fair Trading and cover a wide range of services such as electrical, cleaning, postal, photographic and car repairs. Several of them prohibit the use of exclusion clauses which limit liability for loss or damage – but members of the trade associations have been found to disregard this in a number of cases.

The disadvantage of these codes is that they have no legal force whatsoever and so, if the trade association cannot help resolve your dispute, then you will still have no alternative but to seek your rights under the Supply of Goods and Services Act through legal means. But the codes can be of some help in settling disputes as very often they incorporate some sort of conciliation or arbitration service.

Repairs and Improvements to the Home

There is always a high number of complaints reported to the Office of Fair Trading in this connection. Traders have used high pressure doorstep selling, asked for huge deposits before work is done, and have provided shoddy workmanship, poor service and substandard materials.

Be particularly careful about tradesmen who simply turn up on your doorstep offering to fix your roof or tarmac your driveway. 'We've just noticed you've got some loose slates,' they'll say, helpfully. You may take their word for that, not being in a position, nor having the expertise, to check every nook and cranny of your roof. 'We'll need to ask for something in advance,' may well be the next ploy. 'It's the price of materials today,' they'll say cheerfully. 'Cash flow problems . . . everyone has them.' And suitably sympathetic to the poor man's problem, the unwary householder will hand over a sizeable sum in cash. **Don't**.

When You Choose the Firm

Most of us need to call in a builder at some time or another and since there are plenty of awful reports of half-built extensions and defects which only show up many months afterwards, some sort of guarantee of a firm's reliability is becoming increasingly essential.

One form of protection is to pick a firm which is on the National Register of Warranted Builders, sponsored by the Federation of Master Builders. Any firm which is a member of the Federation has gone through some fairly stringent checks. They will have to show they've been in business for at least three years and three of the recent jobs they've carried out will be inspected for competence and good workmanship. In addition, the firm has to provide all sorts of financial details and references to the Federation.

The scheme is basically insurance. The householder is covered for any defects which might crop up during a two-year period (from when he puts in his bill), as a result of faulty workmanship or materials. The householder should report any faults to the builder and, if he doesn't show any inclination to put things right, then the Federation's arbitration scheme is there to make a decision.

There are certain safeguards, too, should a firm go bankrupt or into compulsory liquidation (but not voluntary liquidation) and the scheme covers actual building work, improvements, repairs, maintenance and decoration up to a total of £25,000.

The cost is an extra 1% on the price – but many firms include this in their bills rather than adding it on. For registered firms in a particular area, contact the National Register of Warranted Builders.

Golden Rules

These are the Office of Fair Trading's seven golden rules for those considering any form of home improvement, whether it's double glazing, roofing, heat insulation, solar heating, gas central heating, plumbing or building.

■ Be clear about requirements before contacting a trader or builder and always have estimates or quotations in writing from at least two firms.

■ Ensure that contracts are written and give full details of prices, cancellation rights, guarantees (including the period of validity) and completion dates.

■ Ensure, by a second opinion, that the firm doing the improvement or repair is competent to carry out the work. Check with someone who has already had work done by the firm – for instance, a neighbour or a friend – and find out whether the firm belongs to a trade association. Members of the Glass and Glazing Federation for instance, work to standards and codes of practice. Most associations will supply a list of their members in your area on request.

■ Be clear exactly who is to carry out the work and whether the supplier, contractor or any sub-contractor is liable if things go wrong.

■ Be careful about paying money in advance or giving unduly high deposits.

■ Shop around and don't be rushed.

■ If a problem does arise, get advice quickly from a solicitor, local Citizens Advice Bureau or Trading Standards Department.

Repairs and Servicing of Domestic Appliances

Any repair should be of a reasonable standard – in other words if someone comes out to fix your tumble dryer or your fridge, you are entitled to expect the appliance will then start working again. Indeed just to be sure, it's always as well, if possible, to try out the appliance before the serviceman leaves your house. It may not be practical to do a full wash, perhaps, but you can certainly switch on a washing machine and give it a quick check for performance, put a record on the stereo to make sure it plays properly or turn the television on to every channel. If you are not satisfied, say so and, if necessary, telephone the repair firm and tell them the fault isn't properly fixed.

Some Safeguards

The Office of Fair Trading was instrumental in setting up Codes of Practice stipulating the standards for the repair and servicing of domestic appliances. So it's always wise to go to one of the firms which belong to the organizations operating these guidelines. The organizations are: The Association of Manufacturers of Domestic Electrical Appliances (AMDEA); Electricity Board shops through-out the UK; and the Radio, Electrical and Television Retailers' Association (RETRA).

The first two deal with 'white goods', namely things like washing machines, spin dryers, refrigerators, toasters, electric cookers and freezers. RETRA also deals with 'brown goods' – radios, televisions, stereo and hi-fi equipment for example.

Points from the Guidelines

■ Servicing and repairs should be quick and efficient. So when you ask for a repair to be done, the initial call will be offered within three working days. If the job can't be finished then (perhaps spares have to be ordered) it should not take more than another 15 days.

■ Spare parts should be fairly easily available – those which are most often asked for should be kept constantly in stock. And, according to the kind of appliance, spares should be available from the manufac-turer for five to 15 years (the longer times for larger appliances such as cookers).

■ Estimates should be provided for those customers who request them.

■ The service or 'call-out charge' should be given when someone requests a repair.

■ Repairs should carry a guarantee. RETRA specify a period of three months and the Scottish Electricity Board three months for labour, 12 months for parts. The receipt acts as evidence of the guarantee – **so get a receipt.**

■ **WARNING:** That's the theory, but the practice is often rather different! Retailers, service agents and electricity boards do not always supply you with an estimate. And, in spite of the code on guarantees, very rarely does one get a written guarantee with a repair – sometimes not even a receipt. Repairmen do not always respond to a call within the three-day time limit, indeed some don't come at all or come at some time other than the one agreed. Spare parts are not always available for as long as they are supposed to be. Or at least that's what customers are told!

The answer is to get copies of the various codes – not the abridged version which appears in the Office of Fair Trading leaflet, but the full version which is surprisingly detailed – from the trade associations concerned, take them along with you when you need a repair and check off all the points. Insist that the service you get corresponds to the one recommended.

Call-out Charges

These probably generate more irritation than almost anything else in the repair game! There are those who don't even realise that there will always be a sum to pay before the chap even lifts a finger. There are those who do expect a charge, but don't expect it to be so large that they will have to ask for an overdraft to pay for it! So what exactly is it?

It's the charge a firm makes for the service engineer to come out to the customer's home and usually includes the first 15 or 30 minutes of his time. After that, his time is charged at a separate hourly rate. The charge varies from a modest £7 to a horrific £30, and covers things like petrol and travelling time.

The codes say a customer should always be 'advised of any minimum charges'. Unfortunately, that rarely seems to happen, so, if we don't want a nasty shock when the bill comes in, it's up to us to get into the habit of asking what the charge is every time we phone a repairer and before we give the go-ahead for him to come out. Shop around – charges vary enormously.

Maintenance Contracts

The alternative to call-out charges is a maintenance contract. This is a form of 'insurance' offered by retailers, manufacturers and service agents. You pay a set sum every year and any repairs required come free of charge. So there are no call-out charges and no expensive parts to pay for. The annual payment varies according to the appliance. Teletext receivers, video recorders and colour televisions are the most expensive (anything from £40 to £50 a year), washing machines and microwave cookers come into the medium price range with vacuum cleaners and fridges about £10 a year or less.

Surveys have tended to show that the frequency and cost of repairs needed on appliances would not justify the annual cost of such a contract and that paying for a repair as it crops up works out more cheaply. But you have to weigh that against the chance of a really major repair being required. For instance, there was a case where a fridge developed a major fault two years after it was purchased and the service agent quoted a call-out fee of £25 plus labour and parts. The householder would probably have found it cheaper to buy a new one or to take out an annual maintenance contract for £8 a year!

So it seems it's all a matter of luck! It's always worth checking on the terms of these contracts, though. One microwave cooker manufacturer, for instance, offers a three-year maintenance contract for the same price as most firms charge for **one year**.

Appointments

'I waited in all day but the chap just didn't turn up.' How often have you heard that? Many people even take time off work and then find the TV repairman doesn't turn up, which is not only irritating but costly, too.

Strictly speaking, when you make an appointment for someone to come to your house to repair an appliance, that agreed time becomes part of your contract. Whichever side breaks it could be liable to pay compensation to the other party. But as with all theories, this one may come a cropper when you try to put it into practice – and who wants to start suing a firm for a broken appointment?

So, to protect yourself, make it very clear at the time you make the appointment what conseqences might result from its not being kept – that you could lose a day's pay, for instance. And follow that up with a confirmation in writing. Then, if the appointment is not kept, you will be able to put the theory into practice by waving the piece of paper at the firm, pointing out they have broken the contract and are liable to pay compensation. Naturally, **you will have kept a copy** of your written confirmation of the time!

Charges

If the TV repairman comes out, looks at your set and says, 'Going to cost a lot this time, madam! More than £50 I reckon to get a new whatsit for the transistorized component . . .' and you decide you'd be better off buying a new set since the one you've got is eight years old – do you have to pay for his coming out?

Yes. The customer must pay call-out charges even if he doesn't give the go-ahead for a repair to be done. The charge covers petrol, maintenance of the van, his time (even while travelling to your house the firm he works for still has to pay him just as much as when he's actually doing a repair) and also covers his time and expertise in telling you what the fault is. And sometimes, even if an appliance is still under guarantee, you may have to pay a call-out charge. It all depends on the terms of the guarantee. So always read it carefully.

When charges are being worked out on an hourly basis it's important to make sure you're not being overcharged. For example, one lady called a plumber. He arrived at her house at 2 p.m., did the job and left again at 2.35 p.m. Yet when the bill came in there was a charge for one and a half hours' labour as well as for the parts.

There's not a lot you can do when that happens, unless you have some way of proving that the chap was actually only in your house for 35 minutes – a witness might be useful. You can, of course, query the bill but, if the firm insists their chap was there for an hour and a half, all you can do is accept defeat gracefully.

Next time take avoiding action! Write down the time when the repairman arrives (just like clocking in at a factory). Get the chap to sign against the time. Note down the time when he leaves the house and get him to sign again. Be sure to use a piece of carbon paper – send one copy to the firm, or give it to the repairman – and keep the other in case your bill is wrong.

Yes, it does take a bit of nerve – but any reputable firm should be glad to go along with that system (indeed it might not be a bad idea if they operated a system like that themselves whereby the householder signed a book to corroborate times of arrival and leaving and that was then used as a basis of sending out accounts). If you do have good grounds to challenge a price, pay the correct rate for the time actually spent and send it with a letter of explanation.

Complaints

If you have a complaint against a firm which is not a member of one of the trade associations mentioned, then, if you cannot resolve it personally, you may have no option but to pursue the matter through the courts.

If you choose a firm which is a member of AMDEA, RETRA or one of the Electricity Boards, then first make a formal complaint by giving the local manager the full details. For unresolved disputes you can then ask for help from the relevant trade association. In the case of Electricity Boards, contact the Electricity Consultative Council for your area. The address will be on your electricity bill in your local showroom and in the telephone directory under 'Electricity'. AMDEA and the Electricity Boards' codes provide for arbitration and a quite independent arbitrator will hear the evidence from both sides and make a decision. RETRA have no arbitration scheme as such but they do have a Conciliation Panel which investigates every dispute and makes a recommendation as to what should be done.

Car Repairs and Servicing

As with any other kind of repair you are entitled to have it carried out in a workmanlike fashion but, if you choose a garage which is a member of either the Motor Agents' Association, the Vehicle Builders' and Repairers' Association, the Society of Motor Manufacturers and Traders or the Scottish Motor Trade Association, then you have some extra protection.

■ **Cost:** A firm quotation should be given if possible or, at the very least, an estimate. It should be made quite clear whether VAT is included.

■ **Extras:** If any stripping or dismantling is necessary before the garage can give a quotation or estimate, you should be told how much you will be charged for this work and whether or not a charge will be made even if you refuse the quotation. If, during the course of the job, it seems as though the original estimate is going to be exceeded, the garage should ask permission before continuing. A quotation, on the other hand, will be binding.

■ **Care:** The garage is bound to take good care of your car and any other possessions which happen to be in it. (It is nevertheless most unwise to leave items in the car!)

■ **Invoices:** These should give the customer full details of all the work carried out and exactly what parts have been used. The date of the repairs should be given on the invoice – as should the mileometer reading at that time.

■ **Guarantee:** Repairs must be guaranteed for a specified number of miles or a period of time. Garages which are members of the VBRA must also guarantee any body repairs they make to a car for either six months or 6,000 miles.

Complaints

In the first instance go to the manager of the local garage and then to the Head Office, if it is a large organization, or the owner, if a small concern. If that fails, get in touch with the relevant trade association. Always make your complaint in writing and enclose copies of any correspondence or documents which you feel are important. Make the complaint within three months.

If you encounter difficulties with a firm which is not a member of one of these associations then, if you are a member of either the AA or the RAC, it would be worth asking their advice and help.

Shoe Repairs

Modern shoes seem to wear out so quickly these days that, unless we're prepared to simply throw away, most of us pay frequent visits to the shoe repairer.

Not all of these belong to a trade association, of course, but a great many do – so look for the symbol if you want the extra safeguards these shops give the customer in terms of service and settling of complaints.

Members of the associations should:

■ Display a list of prices including VAT showing exactly what is offered and what materials are to be used.

■ A ticket must be given to every customer – and it should show the price and the estimated collection date.

■ The workmanship should be good and the result should give satisfactory wear. If it does not, then matters should be put right promptly.

■ Complaints should be dealt with promptly.

The symbols to look out for in shoe repairers (see Chapter Two for the addresses) are: National Association of Shoe Repair Factories and St. Crispin's Boot Trades Association. Keeping an eye on the condition of your shoes and taking them to be repaired before they deteriorate too far can be money well spent.

QUESTIONS TO ASK

What if you lose a repair ticket?

This can be tricky, because really it's your responsibility to look after such things and you can't expect a retailer or repair firm to be specially sympathetic when you've been careless!

Most will, quite rightly, demand proof – otherwise you could simply walk into premises and walk out with something which didn't belong to you. So the best protection one can have in such circumstances is to have full details ready: the precise date you handed in the item for repair, a detailed description of it – colour, size, style, brand name and so on; if it is some sort of gadget or appliance, then have a note of the model number. This may seem like a lot of trouble, but could save you the expense of having to buy something totally new.

Usually the repairer will be able to identify the article and establish to his own satisfaction that you are the rightful owner. But do be prepared to wait a few days to allow them to make a thorough check of the facts, bearing in mind that **they** didn't lose the repair ticket, **you** did!

If you don't collect your property after servicing – what then?

Should you simply not bother to collect your shoes from the repair shop, or your dress from the dry cleaners, can the firm throw out your property, sell it, or charge you a fee for the space it's taking up?

The customer's rights and the firm's responsibility in this matter are clearly set out in legislation introduced in 1977: the Torts (Interference with Goods) Act.

The firm must put the following facts to you **in writing:**
- Where the goods can be collected.
- A description of those goods.
- How much money is due from you.
- A warning that they intend to sell the goods if you don't collect them. (Normally they must give three months notice of any intent to sell, but if there has been a dispute about the price being charged for the service – perhaps that's the reason for the non-collection – then the trader can't sell the goods and can therefore give no notice.)
- **NOTE:** The old laws regarding uncollected goods applied to Scotland, England and Wales – but these were repealed in 1977 when the **new** law came in and this new law **does not** apply to Scotland. The position is much the same in Scotland nevertheless, but one has to fall back on the common law to claim one's legal rights.

Personal Services

Businesses which not only provide workmanship, but materials as well – like a repair to an appliance requiring both parts and labour – make up only one part of the service industry. Others to be found in every High Street offer what might be called a 'pure' service, in the sense that although materials may be used in performance of the service, none are actually supplied to the customer as part of it. We now look more closely at some of these.

Banking

If you have tried to sort out a problem with your local branch manager and the head office with no success, the Banking Ombudsman may be able to help you.

Building Societies

If you think you have suffered financial loss, expense or inconvenience as a result of unfair treatment or maladministration by your building society – and you cannot resolve the matter with the society itself – contact the Building Societies' Ombudsman.

Hairdressing

There has often been pressure on Consumer Ministers to introduce a compulsory registration system for hairdressers, which would give the client some guarantee of skill and reliability but no such system is in operation and no qualifications at all are required to set up in this business.

There is a voluntary registration scheme – but only 30% of hairdressing establishments in the UK are, in fact, registered with the Hairdressing Council (see Chapter Two), which will deal with any complaints against its members. So what steps can you take to gauge the quality of work you can expect in a salon and so avoid some of the 'green hair' situations, which can, unfortunately, arise?

■ Check whether the salon is clean and neat. If the clients seem to be ankle deep in discarded hair clippings or the basins are grubby, then watch out!

■ Look very carefully at any diplomas or documents on the wall which would appear to indicate qualifications. They may be nothing more than proof that the person running the salon has attended a course or demonstration by a hair product manufacturer! Notices on the wall which say 'Member of Hairdressers Federation' or 'Member of Hairdressers Guild' are a pointer to high standards.

■ Don't book a perm or a complicated colour treatment, or anything involving chemicals straight away – start with a simple cut or set to get an idea of the quality of workmanship.

■ If you have a complaint and the hairdresser is not registered with the Hairdressing Council, it is a question of complaining to the hairdressers, or asking your Consumer Advice Centre to take up the matter for you or taking legal advice, if severe damage has been done.

Dry Cleaning

If your clothes come back from the cleaners in a shrunken state or dirty grey when they once were pure white, you naturally tend to blame the cleaner. However, this may not be so. There may be some defect in manufacture which has caused the problem, or you may have used a proprietary stain remover on the material at one point and damaged the surface in some way which only shows up when the dry cleaning process is applied. So don't be too hasty!

If it seems as though the cleaner must be to blame and the firm is a member of the Textile Services Association (TSA) – and 75% are – they should either repair any damage, reclean the article if this will do the trick or pay you fair compensation. What exactly constitutes 'fair compensation' is very much open to interpretation and varies from one firm to another, so much so that the TSA is introducing guidelines for its members to use. However, a deduction will normally be made for wear and tear and you will not get the full replacement value.

TSA members also agree that:

■ they will not use disclaimers – that is, notices which say they can't be responsible for damage to clothes or that articles are left at 'owner's risk'

■ they will pay compensation if something is lost or damaged as the result of fire or burglary while in their care

■ a price list for all standard items should be displayed in the shop

■ any delicate or specially valuable items should be pointed out to the shop assistant, so that it might be sent to Head Office for examination; and a quotation for the work should be given, on request, before going ahead with it

■ delivery times should be kept to.

Complaints

First try to resolve the matter with the shop. If this doesn't produce a result, send details in writing to the TSA's Customer Advisory Service (see Chapter Two). They will try to solve the difficulty and, if they feel it necessary, will arrange for a laboratory test.

Film Processing

We spend some £600 million per year on taking photographs – snapping our family on the beach, at weddings and other family occasions, or recording the local scenery when we go on holiday. However, not every print is perfect. Some are fuzzy, some are too bright, some are too dark and some colours seem to bear little relation to nature. It might be entirely due to our own lack of skill, of course, but it could equally well be the fault of the processor – whether we hand the film to the local High Street chemist or send it off by post.

If prints come to you scratched or if the film is lost or so badly damaged that producing prints is impossible, what are your rights? Generally speaking, if a film is lost, all you would get is a free replacement film. The argument to support this was always that photographs were such an 'intangible' that putting a price on them was impossible and so compensation was either non-existent or minimal. Indeed many film processors made specific claims to the effect that any compensation was limited to the cost of the film itself.

However, in 1981 a photographic firm had to pay £75 compensation for losing a film of a wedding, an occasion which it was obviously not possible to repeat for more photographs! And an award of £100 was made when birthday party celebrations recorded on film were mislaid. So this is a significant step forward in the cause of customers who lose precious prints of a 'once only' occasion, as a result of negligence.

If you have a complaint and the processing firm won't deal with it adequately, then there are trade asociations – the National Pharmaceutical Association and the Association of Photographic Laboratories (see Chapter Two for their addresses). Both of them will take up any dispute on behalf of a customer and the case can be referred to an arbitrator whose decision is legally binding.

Financial Advice

A new regulatory framework was introduced to control the whole area of financial services and investment advice by the Financial Services Act 1986.

A two-tiered framework of self or practitioner based regulation mixed with statutory regulation now exists with the Securities and Investment Board (SIB) in overall supervision under the Department of Trade and Industry.

Below SIB are the recognized professional bodies (RPB) (for solicitors and accountants), recognized investment exchanges and self regulatory bodies (SROs). The self regulatory bodies are
- The Securities Association (TSA)
- The Association of Futures Brokers and Dealers (AFBD)
- Financial Intermediaries, Managers and Brokers Regulatory Association (FIMBRA)
- Investment Management Regulatory Organisation (IMRO)
- Life Assurance and Unit Trust Regulatory Organisation (LAUTRO)

Addresses are in Chapter Two.

From 1988 only individuals authorised by one of the bodies under SIB are able to conduct business. If you seek advice on an investment covered by the Financial Services Act it is your adviser's responsibility to ensure he is properly authorised to give that advice. He is not permitted to advise on other types of investment unless he is specifically authorized. Otherwise he breaks the law.

Investors are well advised to check the registration of advisers they intend doing business with. Just contact the SRO concerned; the list is also on PRESTEL.

Besides the rules governing the way advice is given, investors now have the protection of the Compensation Scheme through SIB. The Scheme will compensate investors up to a ceiling of £48,000 where they have lost money in failed authorized investment businesses.

Complaints about financial services should first be made to the business that handled your investment. Next step, if not satisfied, is to write to the SRO or RPB, step three is write to SIB and finally legal action.

Insurance

Most of us want insurance of some kind – whether it's to cover our home, its contents, our car or even our holidays. So before buying:
- Shop around – policies vary tremendously both in their terms and their price.
- Be wary of words like 'all-in' or 'comprehensive' and similar phrases as you may find you still have to pay an extra premium for a freezer or jewellery or fur coats.

Protection

Those who buy their insurance through a broker have the protection of the Insurance Brokers (Registration) Act. It requires that only those registered with the Insurance Brokers' Registration Council can call themselves 'insurance brokers'. To become registered, a broker must meet professional standards of expertise, qualifications and financial procedures. He also becomes subject to a disciplinary committee which could remove him from the register if he is found guilty of unprofessional conduct or if his entry on the register is fraudulently made. The law regarding registration came into effect on 1 December 1981.

A broker should tell you, if you ask, how much commission he gets on the policies he's offering you. Remember this, and **always ask**!

Insurance Ombudsman Bureau

This was pioneered by some insurance companies and the National Consumer Council in 1981 and it is designed to help policy holders whose complaints remain unresolved after going through the normal process of complaints. The Ombudsman has the power to ask a company to open its books and as a result decides whether or not the client has been treated fairly. If he finds against the company, he can order an award of money to the policyholder.

One drawback is that only those who have policies with insurance companies who are members of the scheme, can ask for help, though an increasing number of companies have joined. If the Ombudsman can't help, he will point enquirers in the direction of whoever can. A brochure on the scheme is available from the Insurance Ombudsman Bureau (see Chapter Two for the address). And it may well pay to pick a company which is a member.

An alternative scheme is the Personal Insurance Arbitration Service (address in Chapter Two) which provides for the settlement of disputes with a number of insurance companies.

Furniture Removers

The 'conditions' which are to be found on every furniture remover's contract can certainly be said to fall into the category of 'small print'! Normally, the conditions are all closely cramped together, in writing so tiny your eyesight has to be perfect to read it and often the print is in colours which makes it even more difficult to pick out. But anyone contemplating a move should read those conditions very carefully indeed before they think of signing the contract.

Watch out, for instance, for the one which says something like: 'Unless otherwise agreed in writing, the Contractors' charges shall be due and payable before the goods are removed, or in the case of goods stored or received for packing, prior to the delivery or removal of the goods etc.' This means in effect that the customer is being asked to pay **in full** and **in advance** for a service on that basis. The removal men argue their case by saying that when they are dealing in every instance with amounts of several hundred pounds they can suffer heavy losses if a cheque bounces – and they claim cheques do – whereas if you pay in advance then the cheque will either be cleared or bounced before they do the job. That guarantees the removal firm their payment, it doesn't necessarily give the customer any guarantees that they will turn up on time and provide an efficient service.

One can understand when a cheque card only guarantees a cheque up to £50 that the companies feel they are at risk. There is nevertheless no need to accept such a condition! Discuss it when the representative comes to your house to work out an estimate, point out that the advance payment makes the whole thing a little too one-sided and suggest alternatives. Either offer a deposit payable in advance, say 10% – that's a more normal way of doing business – or offer a bank reference or give the firm the name and address of your bank and suggest they check for credit worthiness. Again, an acceptable way of doing business. There is no reason at all why these two methods of payment should not be offered, as a matter of course, in the conditions of any removal contract since they are fair to both parties.

It is true to say that other conditions too are outdated! For instance:

The liability of the contractors for any loss, failure to produce or damage shall be limited to either

- the cost of repairing or replacing the damaged or missing article or

■ to TEN POUNDS for any one article, service or complete case or package or other container and the contents thereof (including plate, plated goods and/or other valuables) whichever is the smaller sum.

That means that £10 is the maximum a removal firm is prepared to pay by way of compensation if they lose or damage either one item or a whole packing case full of valuables!

They do offer insurance, of course, to cover loss – but that costs extra. That sort of condition dates back some 30 years or so to the days when £10 might well have been fair compensation and many firms say that every claim for compensation is viewed on an individual basis and they do not usually stick to such a low figure. Such a clause would probably be considered to be invalid under the Unfair Contract Terms Act 1977. So watch out for that condition and take out insurance to be fully protected for damage and loss of your goods.

■ **WARNING:** Always get at least three estimates before choosing any one firm. The price variation is remarkable. For instance, one firm quoted a figure of £245 including insurance and VAT for a removal of some 100 miles whereas another firm quoted £360 plus insurance and VAT for the same job. Contrary to general belief, the larger firms are, generally speaking, **not** the most expensive. In many cases they are the cheapest.

Post Office

Every working day some 30 million letters and half a million parcels are collected and delivered by postmen all over Britain.

As far as the public using the postal service is concerned, there is no actual contract between any individual and the Post Office, so the normal rights of contract don't apply. Nevertheless, the Post Office is legally liable – within set down circumstances – for items which either go missing or are damaged in transit.

A variety of postal methods is available for more valuable items and in some of them a good rate of compensation is available to the customer but even when you use the ordinary letter or parcel post, limited compensation (up to a maximum of £25) is available providing a certificate of posting is obtained.

Complaints

Anyone who is not satisfied with the level of service should contact their local Head Postmaster in the first instance. If a letter or packet has gone missing or has been damaged in some way, then obtain

Form P58 from your Post Office, complete the details required and return it. It's always best to make a claim as soon as possible, since records are only kept for a limited period of time and if the value of an item is in doubt, it's best to enter an estimate of the value on the form and indicate that it is subject to confirmation or change.

If your complaint is not satisfactorily dealt with at local level, the next step is to refer it to the Regional Director. There are ten regions in the UK and the address of yours is to be found at the local Post Office. There are also four Post Office Users' Councils (England, Scotland, Wales and N. Ireland) who can advise on a complaint and perhaps even take it up on your behalf, see Chapter Two.

The Utilities

Privatization of public utilities has introduced new consumer representation and complaint mechanisms in recent years.

Gas and Electricity

The Gas and Electricity Industries have a monopoly and they have a statutory duty to supply. There are, however, certain limits and conditions as far as consumers are concerned.

■ You are entitled to have mains electricity connected providing that your residence is within 50 yards of a main supply point. If you are within 25 yards of a gas main you can ask for a supply but, if for instance you live where no supply is nearby, you have no right to it. Whether or not a supply is made available to a community normally depends on how economic it would prove to be.

■ Your meter, whether gas or electricity, belongs to the board. If you feel it is not giving a correct reading then the board will arrange to have it examined for defects. Servicing of installations is covered under 'Repairs and Servicing of Domestic Appliances' (page 87).

■ A deposit can be asked for before a supply of fuel is given – but this is only normally done when someone has a bad record of paying or is staying on the premises on a temporary basis. As an alternative, the customer can arrange to pay so much every week or month, have a slot meter installed or give an acceptable credit reference or guarantor to the board. Anyone who disagrees with the amount of deposit asked, can have the amount decided by arbitration.

■ Your supply can be cut off for non-payment of bills, but there is a code which says that between October and March it will not be cut off if all those living in the house are old age pensioners and cannot pay, or if the debt is in the name of a past customer. And anyone who is blind, severely sick or disabled, has children under 11 or is getting Income Support will get special consideration in regard to any possible disconnection.

Complaints

Gas: Contact the regional office for your area of the Gas Consumers' Council (address from your bill, showroom or the phone book), or OFGAS (Office of Gas Supply) address in Chapter Two.

Electricity: Contact the Electricity Consultative Council for your area (address from your bill, showroom or the phone book). In Northern Ireland, contact the General Consumer Council for Northern Ireland.

Payment

Most boards offer various ways for the consumer to pay for their fuel apart from in one lump sum. You can pay an agreed amount each week or month towards the bill, buy savings stamps at showrooms, pay what you like when you like towards your next bill, have a slot meter installed or pay a set amount every month (estimated on your year's consumption) by standing order through your bank. Token meters for gas and electricity are gradually being introduced to offer an alternative to coin meters.

Telephone Service

Many subscribers would like a meter in the house as with gas and electricity, so that they could check their own phone bills, but British Telecom say this is not practical.

If you feel you are being overcharged you can ask for it to be checked. Each subscriber's meter at the exchange is read and the readings photographed in batches then transferred to a computer. Small rural exchanges may still be on a manual reading system. Any bill which adds up to more than twice the previous one is automatically checked before sending out.

Self-Help to Avoid Overcharging

- If you get a wrong number ring the operator and ask for a credit.
- Don't listen in to other conversations on a crossed line – however fascinating they may be – you could be charged for the calls if they are registering on your meter! So, if this happens, put the phone down.
- A receiver which is not correctly returned to its position after a call

might mean you are still being charged for the call for some minutes, even after the person on the other end has hung up.

What Services are on Offer?

■ Credit calls – for an extra charge you can get a card which allows you to make calls – always through the operator, though – from a phone other than your own and the calls are charged to your own number.

■ When you go on holiday you can't stop your cleaning lady or your neighbours using the phone when they come in to feed the cat. For a fee you can have the service temporarily suspended. A lockable phone to prevent outgoing calls is also available for an extra quarterly fee.

■ You can change your phone number if the one you've got is similar to the local pub's for instance – for a small fee.

■ You can get a subscriber's meter fitted but British Telecom says it cannot guarantee its accuracy and it costs rental every quarter plus an installation charge. You can also get an extra-long flex as well as amplifying equipment if disabled, again for a fee.

Complaints

The British Telecom Code of Practice for Consumers is set out in your phone book. If you want to complain about an extortionate phone bill or other BT service you should first contact your area office (address on your phone bill), then the local Telecommunications Advice Committee (TAC), if there is one. Advice will also be given by the Secretary of the appropriate National Advisory Committee on Telecommunications (the addresses are at the back of your phone book).

You may also contact OFTEL (Office of Telecommunications) address in Chapter Two.

Mercury

In competition with BT, Mercury is enlarging its telephone network and its number of domestic subscribers is growing.

Budget Accounts

These are a good way to pay for fuel and other regular household bills. You work out how much the annual payments for the various items will be – add on a little extra for the inevitable price increases – then the total is divided by 12 and that amount is paid monthly into a special budget account from your current bank account. Bills are then paid from that account. Different banks charge differently for this facility (and one even pays interest on your credit balance).

Buses and Trains

You have a contract with the organization – in other words you pay them a certain sum of money and in consideration of that they deliver you to wherever you are going. And as with most contracts, there are conditions attached. They won't all be detailed on your ticket but there will be a note to the effect that the conditions are available on request at the booking office.

British Rail has no absolute responsibility to carry you by a particular train or to ensure you don't miss connections or suffer delays – so you can't claim unless you could prove negligence in some way. Timetables are more in the nature of a 'broad guide', not a promise that trains will leave and arrive precisely when stated.

Of course, if a train can't complete its journey, you would get expenses incurred in getting to your destination by other means – normally the railway would try to arrange alternative transport.

To travel ticketless would be an offence only if you did it quite deliberately to avoid payment. If you go first class with a second-class ticket then you can be asked to pay the difference.

In the case of personal injury both rail and bus companies will compensate passengers. And in the event of luggage or other property being lost or damaged, compensation will be made on the basis indicated on the conditions of carriage, available to the public.

Complaints

They should be taken first to local area managers but, if the dispute isn't resolved, then in the case of railways, refer it to the Transport Users' Consultative Committee (your local one) and, in the case of buses, to the Headquarters' address shown in timetables.

Air Travel

As with other transport services, an airline ticket is subject to certain conditions. Those relating to the airline's liability to passengers in case of death or injury and damage to baggage are mostly a matter of an international agreement called the Warsaw Convention.

There are certain financial limits on liability and these can vary according to whether the flight is domestic or international. Conditions on an airline timetable or ticket cannot in any way affect the passenger's rights in regard to negligence.

Delays

The general position here is that an airline is not liable providing all reasonable steps have been taken to prevent delays. Bad weather preventing take-off, cannot, for instance, be prevented, nor can industrial action.

One form of delay can be caused by overbooking – more commonly known as 'bumping' in the trade. Some people make several different seat reservations on flights, but only take up one of them, thus leaving 'no shows' (empty seats). To compensate for this, airlines may book more passengers than they have seats on a flight to accommodate but if their calculations are wrong, some passengers may have to be 'bumped' on to another flight with a delay, in some cases, of 24 hours. Many airlines now operate a scheme whereby they offer compensation in accordance with a fixed scale. In America, there is a mandatory system and the level of compensation is higher.

The Air Transport Users' Committee (see Chapter Two), the watchdog body representing passenger interests in the UK, have long recognized this problem and hope that levels of compensation in Europe may be increased.

Luggage

Conditions affecting the carriage of luggage by air are included in the international agreements already mentioned. In the case of loss or damage while luggage is in the airline's care, liability is limited to about £12 per kilo – except in those cases where the passenger has declared the value of his baggage to be of a certain amount and has paid an extra charge. Hand luggage which is normally kept on the plane, is also subject to a limit.

Checking out Conditions

Always read the conditions on tickets carefully and if you want any further clarification or information, then ask for full details at the airline office.

Taxis and Mini Cabs

- Taxis are licensed by their local authority, therefore there are sometimes individual bye-laws covering them.
- The cabbie's licence number must be displayed both at the rear of the taxi and in the passenger compartment.
- Taxis must have adequate insurance in terms of passenger risk.
- If a taxi driver is in an authorized cab rank, he must accept the first person waiting in the rank.
- Taxi fares are controlled and the charge must be shown on the meter.
- Even if showing a 'For Hire' sign, a taxi driver doesn't have to stop if you hail him in the street.

Mini cabs are not licensed at all and therefore they are not subject to the same controls as licensed taxis.

Complaints

Always take a note of the taxi's licence number and get in touch with the local licensing authority.

Public transport at local level is often operated by a number of different organizations. In case of complaint, the best plan is to consult the timetable for information on where the complaints should be lodged. The address and phone number of the local office are usually given.

Health Services

For routine care under the National Health one must be registered with a local general practitioner. Everyone has the right to be on a GP's list. Lists of doctors are available in post offices, from Family Practitioner Committees (in England and Wales) and local Health Councils (in Scotland), quite apart from Citizens Advice Bureaux everywhere.

If you can't find a doctor who will accept you on his list (and many have huge lists already), then in England and Wales, the Family Practitioner Committee will find you one and in Scotland you should approach the local health board (under 'Health' in the telephone directory), which has an obligation to help you find a doctor.

Your Rights

■ If you go along to your doctor's surgery, he is obliged to see you, unless there is an established appointment system and you simply haven't bothered to make one. You could be asked to make an appointment but, if you are in urgent need of treatment, then it would be up to the doctor to decide whether a later appointment would be a risk to your health.

■ Home visits are not necessarily available 'on demand'. It is entirely up to the doctor to decide whether one is required or not.

■ If you are away from home, contact any GP in the area. If your stay is up to three months you can get on a local GP's list on a temporary basis.

■ In an emergency a hospital casualty department will treat you.

■ You have the right to change your doctor without giving any reason for doing so. If you can't get another yourself then send a card to your local Health Board in Scotland and your Family Practitioner Committee in England and Wales.

Hospitals

Except in an emergency, you can't generally just go into a hospital and ask for treatment – you need to be referred there by your GP. You are also not able to choose which hospital you'd like to go to.

Normally you can leave hospital if you choose to do so. You can only be refused permission to leave if you have a longstanding or infectious disease or under the Mental Health Act.

Is Treatment Always Free?

In general, routine treatment either at your GP's surgery or in hospital is free but GPs can charge for sickness certificates, examinations for insurance policies or certain vaccinations required if going abroad.

Hospitals can charge for amenity or 'pay' beds.

A charge is made for prescriptions unless the patient is pregnant, or has had a baby in the previous 12 months, is on Income Support or Family Credit, is either under 16 or over the retirement age, between 16 and 18 and in full-time education, receiving a war or service disablement pension and needing prescriptions for the disability, or suffering from one of certain medical conditions. Some people on low income may also be entitled to free prescriptions.

Complaints

For advice about this, go to the local Community Health Council in England and Wales and the local Health Council in Scotland. If you have a complaint about a hospital then these councils will be able to advise on how to set about it.

If you are not happy with the outcome of a complaint at local level you can send the details of it to the 'Ombudsman', more properly known as the Health Service Commissioner. The complaint must go to him within a year, and can only be dealt with if it concerns the way services are administered or the lack of proper services.

Dentists

Unlike a doctor, a dentist is an independent contractor and is paid on a sort of 'piece work' arrangement.

■ Explain clearly that you want the work done under the NHS or you may be charged. For each treatment a form has to be signed by the patient – so if you don't get a form, ask why not. It is up to the patient to establish his NHS rights.

■ Usually work can be done without reference to the Dental

Estimates Board but some specialist treatment may require approval.
- Dentists are under no obligation to carry out any NHS treatment if they don't want to. You can chop and change dentists as often as you want, so simply go to another one.
- Not all preventitive dentistry is available on the NHS.
- Free dental treatment is available to those under 17, pregnant women and women who have had a baby in the previous 12 months, those on Income Support or Family Credit, and young people aged 18 in full-time education.
- Some people on low income may be entitled to help with the cost.

Complaints

First take your complaint to the dentist who carried out the treatment. If things are not resolved with him then the next stage would be to contact your local health authority.

Optical Care

Anyone who feels they may be in need of glasses or some other eye care, can simply make an appointment with an optician of their choice. Although it may often be one's GP who recommends a visit to the optician, a letter from him is no longer required for an appointment, as was once the case. A free eye test is available to those under 16, on Income Support or Family Credit, between 16 and 18 in full-time education, people who need complex lenses, people who are registered blind or partially sighted, people with diabetes or glaucoma, or people aged 40 or over who are the parent, brother, sister or child of someone with glaucoma. Some people on low income may get help with costs.

Having got a prescription, you can then choose between:
- Lenses and frames both from the NHS.
- NHS lenses fitted into commercially-produced frames.

Ophthalmic opticians are qualified in all aspects of eye care – they can examine eyes and issue prescriptions, but you don't necessarily have to get your glasses fitted there – instead you can look around and go to a 'dispensing optician' whose qualifications only allow him to fit glasses.

Since 1981, opticians have been allowed to display the prices of spectacle frames and lenses in their windows – the intention being that the customer would have more chance to shop around, compare prices and get a better deal all round.

Contact lenses can only be prescribed on NHS in certain cases.

Complaints

Complaints should be taken to the Community Health Council or local Health Council (in Scotland) for advice.

EIGHT

SELLING

Shops represent the traditional way of buying things and most of us probably spend a fair proportion of our budget buying this way. But we spend money buying goods in other ways, too. We may go to an auction, or send off for something we see in a magazine advertisement or buy a shower or a set of books in our own living room. So let's look at these different methods of selling and what rights and protection the customer has.

Auctions

Broadly speaking, there are two types of auctions. The first, the specialist auction, deals only in a particular thing like stamps or wine or paintings. The second has a selection of miscellaneous articles, which can include anything from jewellery to cutlery. When you buy at an auction you may well get a fantastic bargain, but you could just as easily end up with a load of rubbish. You take a risk and the transaction is not a 'consumer sale' in the normal sense of the phrase – usually leaving you with no rights in terms of faulty goods. The Conditions of Sale which auctioneers work to almost always take away your legal rights and you simply have to accept the fact.

'*By making a bid the bidder automatically acknowledges his acceptance of the conditions of sale*' is a commonly used principle in the auction room.

Other points you will find incorporated into the Conditions of Sale are '*The auctioneers act as agents only*' – that means they can't be held responsible if anything goes wrong; and '*Every lot in the sale is sold with all faults and errors of description. The auctioneers have no liability, nor does the vendor, for authenticity, age, origin, condition or quality of the said articles.*' That's back to the medieval principle of '*let the buyer beware*' – so if your judgement is wrong then too bad, because you can't rely on what either the auctioneer or the catalogue tells you as being necessarily so! However, if you feel that it is unreasonable for an auctioneer to rely on a condition denying responsibility, it is always open to you to challenge this in court under the Unfair Contract Terms Act.

'If a dispute should arise among bidders, the auctioneer has total discretion to settle it or re-offer that particular lot if he so decides.' That means you accept his decision like it or not.

The Trade Descriptions Act does in fact apply to descriptions of sale goods as written in the catalogue. But few cases have ever been brought under the Act. And what one must remember is that, even if a Trading Standards Officer did bring a prosecution and the firm were fined as a result, there is no guarantee that the customer would get any financial recompense. So the rules are:

■ Try to get to the preview and examine any articles you like very carefully.

■ Check the conditions of sale.

■ Be prepared to pay cash or at least 25% by way of a deposit and the rest soon afterwards.

■ Ask what the delivery charge is and what the time limit is for removing goods. Sometimes the conditions are that unless purchases are removed they can be resold and all you'll get back is exactly what you paid for them.

■ If you find you have made a bid for the wrong lot and get it – then tell the auctioneer's clerk as soon as you can. You may be lucky and it will be re-offered but the auctioneer has no obligation to do so.

■ The auctioneer does not have to accept the highest bid (or indeed any bid) and the item can be withdrawn if its reserve price is not reached.

■ It's at the precise moment the hammer hits the desk that your offer is accepted and you are bound to go ahead with the purchase.

Car Auctions

Quite a lot of people go along to their local car auction these days if they want a second-hand car, and, as with all auctions, there are bangers to be had and there are bargains. Sometimes almost new models sell for thousands less than you'd pay in a car dealer's showroom. However, you have very few rights of redress if anything goes wrong if you're tempted to buy this way. These are some points to remember.

■ There is a viewing period before every sale so make use of it, if possible taking along an expert to look at the car. You normally have until noon the following day if you want to have the vehicle checked over.

■ Good firms of auctioneers will give a warranty which covers mechanical bits and pieces but does not cover bodywork.

■ The auctioneer will normally check with the Hire Purchase Information Centre in Salisbury before the sale – just to establish that there's no loan outstanding, or that the car hasn't been an insurance write-off.

■ What if the car later turns out to be stolen? A good auctioneer will offer an indemnity against this and the charge for the insurance involved is added to the price of the car. The premium is approximately £6 for a car costing up to £1,000 and £2 for every £1,000 above that price. This means that, should the police turn up and take the car away, you'll lose the car, but you will get your money back.

One-day Sales and Auctions

These are held up and down the country, in village halls, hotels and even pubs. Some sales are genuine, but others are not and these are the ones to watch out for – the ones Trading Standard officers constantly get complaints about from unwary consumers who have been conned. They usually spring up quite suddenly. Notices appear outside a hall overnight or people push leaflets into the hands of High Street shoppers which advertise the 'sale of the century' taking place in a couple of hours' time. The aim is to make a quick kill – relying on the gullibility of the customer to make a lot of money – then they move on just as quickly as they appeared, leaving no trace or forwarding address!

The goods being offered for sale might be described as bankrupt stock on the leaflets and advertising posters the organizers put out but in reality they're more likely to be rubbish no respectable retailer would ever dream of selling! Even worse, some of the items might be downright dangerous, so always be especially wary of buying electrical goods this way. Other goods may be in packages with well-known brand names written on the **outside** of the wrapping, but the goods **inside** might not carry the same name. The trick to gain confidence is for the salesman to offer small things at ridiculous prices – Biro pens for one penny and so on. People are then convinced they are getting bargains – they've taken the bait! 'Plants' among the audience then start to bid for whatever is being offered – only this time the prices are £20 and over.

When customers get their goods home they discover them to be shoddy rubbish, but by that time the salesmen have moved on, with their pockets full of money.

There were so many complaints from consumers about these sales that the Office of Fair Trading introduced a nationwide code to encourage any public house, hotel or hall who had accepted a booking for such sales, to notify their local Trading Standards Office and allow them to check out the organizers.

How to Spot the Cowboys

■ Look for the name and address of the firm organizing the sale. If there is no such information on posters, leaflets or whatever, then be wary. Before you go along to the sale itself ask whoever owns the pub, hotel or hall, if they can tell you who the organizers are.

■ Say you'd like a chance to look at the goods before you buy. If this is refused – go home!

■ Watch out for a common trick used at such sales: the goods are offered at a price (say £10) and then a refund of say £8 is offered if you buy. Only the 'plants' in the crowd actually get the refund – you don't!

Mail Order

In any one year, approximately 40% of the UK population buys something by mail order. (Scotland, in fact, tops the list, with England next, then Wales and Northern Ireland.)

For those who live a long way from shops or for housewives who also have a job to cope with, it can be a real boon. However, there can be all sorts of problems, too! Surveys show that something like 12% of us encounter difficulties.

■ 'I've written to the book club three times to tell them that I have never received the book but they just keep sending me bills for it.'

■ 'Six weeks ago I sent off for a dress I saw in one of those glossy colour adverts. I've written twice but received no reply – and the party I planned to wear the dress to was last week.'

These are typical of the two most common areas of complaint – mix-ups over payment, colour, size or style of the goods ordered and late delivery. So let's look at the different ways of 'buying by post' – four ways in all – and what protection the consumer has in each case.

Catalogues

Most of the largest firms who trade this way belong to the Mail Order Traders' Association and follow its code of practice agreed with the Office of Fair Trading. So it's wise, when you get a catalogue, to look for the code of practice statement.

Some of the points from the MOTA code:

- The information given in the catalogue about the size, colour, materials, installation and any restrictions on use will be spelled out clearly and accurately alongside the article.
- You don't have to pay for goods until you actually get them and then you have 14 days to decide whether to keep them or not and, if you decide to keep them, you can pay for them either with a single payment or in instalments of usually 20 or 38 weeks.
- **WARNING:** Be careful that you do not exceed the 14-day 'on approval' period because, if you are late in returning goods, the firm would be quite right to refuse to take them back and to ask for payment.
- Delivery dates quoted will be met and, if not, you can cancel and get your money back.
- Any surcharges and restricted availability of goods should be clearly detailed and, if you live in an area where there are additional delivery charges, these should be given.
- The firm will give details of servicing arrangements which are available for any goods which would require them, such as domestic appliances, if the customer asks for them.

Complaints

MOTA offers a conciliation service for customers who can't get their complaints resolved by the firm concerned. And, if conciliation fails to produce a satisfactory settlement, customers will be pointed towards a low-cost arbitration service. This acts as an alternative to going to court and you won't normally have to appear yourself. The problem will be dealt with using written evidence only – a good reason for always keeping documents and correspondence.

So if you have a complaint, first ask the agent to sort it out for you. If that fails, write to the catalogue company yourself and, if that doesn't solve the problem, get in touch with the Mail Order Traders' Association.

Postal Bargains

There must be thousands of advertisements in newspapers and magazines every week, ranging from small box-type ads in black and white to the glossy, colour ones which fill a whole page. What they all have in common is that they are offering goods for sale whether it's a silk blouse or a kitchen gadget. So many different companies sell by post in this way that there is no one association covering them all. So in that sense, you're on your own, but there are certain safeguards.

The British Code of Advertising Practice applies to any trader who advertises in any newspaper or magazine. If you pay money in advance the advertiser is obliged, under the code, to refund your money if you return the goods undamaged within seven days of receiving them. He must also refund your money if the goods are not delivered within 28 days and you decide you no longer want them. The exception to this is if the advertisement specifies a waiting period of more than 28 days so that you ordered the goods on that basis. The following points should also be observed:

■ Any refund should be made just as soon as the firm receives the goods you have returned.

■ Credit notes are **not** an acceptable alternative to a refund.

■ If goods are damaged or if they are not as described (for instance, if the dress is not the colour you ordered), the customer is entitled to be refunded the postage he pays for sending back the goods.

■ Orders should be delivered within 28 days, with the exception of plants and made-to-measure goods. If the trader can't deliver within that time he must inform you, thus giving you the choice of a refund.

■ **WARNING:** Remember that the Advertising Code of Practice is purely voluntary and cannot be enforced by law. However, the Advertising Standards Authority will investigate any complaint and contact the firm involved to get their side of the story. If they feel the firm is in breach of the code, they may ask the firm to withdraw the ad or change it and the complaint will be published in ASA reports.

The Mail Order or Readers' Protection Scheme is another safeguard when you buy directly from an advertisement. It is operated by the various publications themselves to ensure that their readers don't lose money if one of the advertisers goes out of business.

■ **WARNING:** This protection **does not** apply:

■ When the advert appears under a 'classified ads' head.

■ You have not ordered the goods **directly** from the advert but have sent off for a brochure or leaflet advertised and then ordered from that.

But with the exception of those two circumstances, if you send off money in answer to an advertisement, but no goods are delivered, no refund of your money is offered and no explanation given, this is what you do under the Mail Order Protection Scheme:

■ Write to the firm you ordered the goods from, asking why they have not been delivered.

■ If you hear nothing, write to the Advertisement Manager of the newspaper or magazine in which the advertisement appeared. Give the date of the advertisement, the date of your order, what you ordered, the amount you paid and details of any receipt you have.

■ If the firm has gone bankrupt or into liquidation, you will be told.

- In that event, submit a formal claim to the publication, including some proof of payment.
- All being in order, your money will be refunded.

If the advertisement was in a magazine, then claims must be submitted within two months of your order, if in a newspaper within three months of the date of the paper.

Book and Record Clubs

Most of the firms who sell in this way belong to the Association of Mail Order Publishers and they all work to a Code of Practice which affords customers some protection when difficulties arise. It covers not only books, but records and cassettes. So look for the symbol of AMOP – the code may not be perfect but it does at least give you a course of action should problems crop up.

These are some of the points of the code:
- Information about how many books you must order, how much they will cost and how often you will be required to order a book, must be made clear.
- When you agree to buy a number of books or records over a fixed period of time, you can cancel the agreement either after 12 months or if prices rise more than you were told they would.
- No 'free approval' claims should be made if the customer has to pay the cost of the return postage.
- No goods must be sent unless the customer orders them.
- Despatch dates will be given when payment is asked for in advance.
- Any delays should be explained.
- Debt collection will be reviewed regularly to make sure that no customer is bothered unless there is a very sound basis for it.

Complaints

First write to the Customer Service Department. If you still get demands for payment for books you didn't order then the next step is to write to the Mail Order Publishers' Authority who will try to sort out any problem concerning one of its members. What one must remember is that most firms in this line of business use computers for all their records – but computers only do what human beings tell them to. So, don't blame the computer, write to the person who instructs it!

Direct Mail

This is literature of one kind or another pushed through the letterbox or delivered in bulk by the Post Office, its aim being to persuade you to buy the firm's products. It is a growth industry and is, apparently, a successful way of selling, according to the firms which use this method.

There is a British Direct Mail Marketing Association (BDMA) which is setting up a Code of Practice in conjunction with the Office of Fair Trading and which will have a conciliation service for anyone who has a complaint against a member company. Members of the BDMA follow the normal rules associated with the Code of Practice issued by the Advertising Standards Authority – the same rules which apply to other forms of selling.

Many people do find it intensely irritating to get a lot of unwanted paper through the letterbox and the Advertising Standards Authority and the Consumers' Association have from time to time been concerned about any possible nuisance this may cause. Firms can run the risks too, of losing potential customers if they annoy them by sending unwanted literature. So the ASA suggests that firms carefully scrutinize their mailing list before they send out any material and make an effort to remove from it the namesof anyone who has written asking that this be done.

A clearing house has been set up (the Mailing Preference Service, see Chapter Two for the address), so that the public will have **one** address to write to – just one letter saying we do not want any unsolicited mail. A computer will then take over and make sure that those companies using this form of selling are aware of our wishes.

Complaints

Any difficulties arising out of direct mail should be referred to the British Direct Mail Marketing Association (see Chapter Two).

Unsolicited Goods

This practice, once common, is now controlled by legislation (Unsolicited Goods and Services Act 1971 and 1975). The trick was simply to send goods to people who hadn't ordered them and whose names were taken at random. The sales material with the goods indicated that one must either pay for them or return them within a certain period of time – and if return was not made during the seven or 14 days allowed, payment would be due!

Consumers who ignored such claims were sometimes sent threatening letters and demands for payment were common. Concern among consumer organizations led to the introduction of legislation.

■ It is now an offence for traders to demand payment for goods which are sent to people who haven't ordered them in the first place.

- If you receive goods you didn't ask for and you don't want them you can simply keep them and during a period of six months from receipt of the goods the onus is on the firm concerned to collect them from you.

- You can cut short the six-month period by writing to the sender giving your name and address and stating that the goods were not asked for and that you do not want them. If the sender has not taken them back within 30 days, the goods become your property.

- There is no obligation at all for someone who gets goods they didn't ask for, to enter into any correspondence regarding them or to send back the goods at his own expense. If, however, a firm sends the postage and requests the return of the goods it would seem unreasonable not to do so.

Since 1975, further legislation protects the consumer even more in regard to demands for payment. The Unsolicited Goods and Services (Invoices, etc.) Regulations 1975 says that any note of price or invoice sent with goods which were not ordered, must contain two prominent notices in RED:

- 'This is not a demand for payment and there is no obligation to pay'.

- 'This is not a bill'.

There is a maximum penalty of £400 if the sender threatens to bring legal proceedings.

Telephone Selling

This sales technique, imported from the United States, is being used more and more as a means of reaching consumers. The only safeguards the telephone subscriber has at the moment in regard to 'sales calls' are the guidelines of professional standards and ethics which are set out by the British Direct Marketing Association. These are:

- Telephone presentations should be clear and honest.
  - □ There should be no attempt to mislead, exaggerate or to use partial truths.
  - □ Sales calls should not be made in the guise of research or a survey.
  - □ Normal rules of telephone courtesy should be used and high pressure tactics avoided.
  - □ The caller should provide the person called with a clear opportunity to accept or decline the offer.

- Telephone calls to consumers should be made during reasonable hours, bearing in mind that what is regarded as reasonable could vary in different parts of the country and in different types of household. Should a call have occurred at a time inconvenient for the customer, an offer to call back at a more convenient time should be made.

■ Any enquiries concerning the source of the potential customer's or donor's name and/or telephone number and any other requested information regarding the telephone call should be clearly answered.

  □ Conscientious effort should be made to remove callers' names from contact lists when requested to do so.

  □ Unlisted or unpublished numbers should not be called.

■ The caller should give his name and the name of the person and/or organization responsible for the call campaign and repeat this information upon request at any time during the conversation. The latter name and address should, therefore, appear in the telephone directory (or, if a new number, be obtainable through Directory Enquiries) to enable the person called to verify the authenticity of the caller.

■ Telephone calls should be made within the prevailing legal framework. Care should be taken to ensure that telephone orders are not accepted from minors without adult approval.

So what should you do in the event that you receive a telephone sales call?

First, make sure you get a note of the name and address of the firm the caller claims to be representing. Then look it up in the telephone directory (ask the caller to wait until you do so). If all the information given by the caller in regard to name, address and phone number does not correspond to that given in the directory, then be very wary.

If you do have any cause for complaint (and callers have been known to try high pressure techniques or say the call is part of a survey being carried out in a particular area), then telephone or write to the Head Office of the company the caller represents, giving full details. If you don't want any more calls, tell them so. If you do not get a satisfactory explanation (or perhaps apology) from the firm concerned, then contact the British Direct Marketing Association, see address in Chapter Two. The firm concerned may not, of course, be a member, but it's worth trying.

Doorstep Selling

There are many worthwhile firms selling useful and well-made products to us on our own doorsteps – that no one would deny. But, equally, there are quite a few less scrupulous salesmen who will tell any tale to persuade us to buy something we don't need and can't afford.

So, first, spot the salesman. Many of the ploys they use are so well worn that the Office of Fair Trading compiled a list of the most common. These are some examples:

- 'I'm selling on behalf of the blind/disabled/old age pensioners . . .'
- 'I've been sent by the council/social security/gas/electricity board .'
- 'If you'd like to cut your fuel bills, I can help you do it . . .'
- 'I'm just doing some market research in your area . . .'
- 'I'm a consultant on back problems . . .'
- 'Good morning, madam, it's your lucky day because your house has been chosen as a showhouse for your area . . .'

The counterattack is:

- Ask the person to produce identity. Any genuine official carries an identity card and is quite happy to produce it.
- Today almost all 'official' market researchers belong to a scheme launched by the Market Research Society and that means they have a numbered card bearing their photograph and the name and address of the company they represent.
- Even someone who actually admits to being a salesman should be asked for identity – someone from a reputable company will supply this information immediately and the name, address and telephone number should be on any promotional material he may show you.

The golden rules to remember:

- Don't be taken in by claims that you are being offered a special discount providing you buy immediately. The 'discount' is being offered to everyone in the street and it's a fairly safe bet that you'll get it whenever you buy.
- Never think of buying anything on the doorstep until you have checked around the shops for comparative prices.
- Don't ever say 'yes' on the spot. Even if you are genuinely interested in the product, always ask the salesman to leave you information and literature. If he's genuine he'll be happy to come back the next day for your custom.
- Ask if the firm is a member of a trade association. The Direct Selling Association (DSA) which sells goods this way has a code of conduct. It says that sales reps should not ask for full payment in advance for any products. So don't ever hand money over before goods are delivered. The code also says that DSA members will give receipts for money received and will abide by guarantees to give refunds on deposits. The Glass and Glazing Federation (members sell double glazing) have their own code of practice – so if you do want double glazing, ask if the representative's firm is a member. Their code gives improved rights of cancellation. And if it's solar heating the chap's selling, ask if his firm is a member of the Solar Trade

Association. It runs a conciliation and arbitration service to deal with customer complaints and there is a new British Standard for solar heating installations.

■ **WARNING:** Remember to ask for some proof that the firm is actually a member of a trade association. If the salesman simply says 'yes' you've no way of checking the authenticity of the statement without seeing a letterhead or something similar indicating membership.

Signing an Agreement

If you have decided to go ahead and buy, always read the document very carefully before you sign – and that means the small print in particular!

■ **Be tough** with the doorstep sellers – they are slick and trained to reel off a sales script to perfection!

■ **Be rude** if one is unduly persistent – there have been instances of salesmen still trying to persuade a family to buy a product when the clock was striking midnight.

■ **Be suspicious** of all claims and never take them at face value without checking.

■ **Be wary** of even letting a salesman get a foot past your front door unless you really do need whatever he's selling. Don't sign anything without first reading it carefully. If you don't understand it, don't sign and never ever sign a form unless all the relevant details have been entered on it and checked by you as being accurate.

Party Plan Selling

This is 'in house' selling rather than 'on the doorstep' but it's still direct selling. Again, the idea began in America and now you can buy everything from kitchenware to underwear by party plan.

You are asked along to a party at a friend or neighbour's house. The firm's products are shown and demonstrated and you are invited to place an order. It's in the nature of a social event and some of the firms' hostesses organize games for guests as well as providing coffee and biscuits. One of the games usually offers a sample product as a 'prize'.

Advantages: On the whole, the goods offered are of good quality and you do have the personal contact with the person selling them (he or she usually lives locally) so there's a contact in case of complaint. It can be a convenient way of buying for those with young children because the 'parties' are often held in the evenings when babysitters are available.

Disadvantages: People can feel bound to place an order so as not to be thought mean by their friends and neighbours. So don't go to a party in the first place if you are not prepared to buy. It's therefore essential to find out before you go along exactly what kind of goods are being sold.

■ Guests at the party will be entitled to cancellation rights on purchases or orders over £35.

■ Make sure you know the name and the address of the company who is supplying the goods.

■ Send off for a free leaflet called 'Shopping at Home' which is published by the Direct Selling Association, the organization to which most firms selling by party plan belong. Enclose a stamped, addressed envelope for the leaflet.

■ Your rights concerning faulty goods are the same as for goods bought in any other way. You should first complain to the agent selling them. If he or she cannot sort it out, then write to the DSA. Members of this association work to a code of practice which says that customers should have two weeks in which to change their mind about goods ordered and get their deposit refunded. Also that sales leaflets must show the firm's name and address.

■ If problems do arise about any firm which is a member of the DSA, then write to the association with details.

NINE

HOLIDAYS

A holiday which one hopes will bring relaxation and enjoyment, does not represent good value for money if the whole thing turns into one long torture of overbooking, delays and disappointments. So, how do you prevent a dream holiday from becoming a nightmare? The answer is three-fold:

- Careful advance planning
- Checking that ubiquitous small print
- Knowing your rights and how to put them into practice

Before Booking
Once you have decided which country and perhaps which particular resort you'd like to go to, get hold of as many holiday brochures as you possibly can. You'll find that taking the same holiday, on the same dates, in the same hotel and getting exactly the same food and accommodation terms can vary in cost by as much as £50 *per person* depending on the tour operator offering the holiday.

Check on extra charges
- ☐ Are meals included in the package?
- ☐ Do children go free or at a reduced price?
- ☐ How much will the insurance be?
- ☐ Is the price of travel from airport to hotel included?
- ☐ Is there an extra supplement for a single room?
- ☐ Is the charge per person or per room?

Check on amenities
- ☐ How far from the beach is the hotel?
- ☐ How far are the local shops and public transport?
- ☐ Is the beach sand or shingle?
- ☐ Are there any special facilities for children?
- ☐ Does the room have a view?
- ☐ Do you have your own bath/shower?
- ☐ Are there any steep slopes, awkward for the elderly?
- ☐ If the brochure only shows an artist's impression of the hotel, check that the building has been completed.

Brochures

These must observe the requirements of the Trade Descriptions Act (which means that all statements must be accurate and in no way misleading to the customer), the Misrepresentation Act (this does not apply in Scotland) and the Civil Aviation Act 1971. In regard to the Trade Descriptions Act a travel agent or tour operator cannot be held liable for statements which he believed to be true at the time he made them.

In addition to these legal requirements, there is a Code of Practice drawn up by the Association of British Travel Agents (ABTA), see Chapter Two for the address, in conjunction with the Office of Fair Trading and, in regard to brochures, that code specifies as follows:

■ Every brochure published by, or in the name of, the operator, shall contain clear, comprehensive and accurate information to enable the client to exercize informed judgement in making a choice including:

■ The means of travel – ship, air, train or whatever
■ The destination and/or itinerary, if applicable
■ The dates, times and places of departure and return
■ The nature of accommodation and meal facilities
■ Any additional facilities or arrangements included in the holiday
■ The total price, together with a statement of the services included and also the date on which the price is calculated and the conditions under which it can be amended
■ The booking conditions

Booking

The booking conditions for whatever type of holiday, whether in a hotel or self-catering, booked through an ABTA travel agent must be set out clearly, and be accurate and conform to the ABTA Code of Practice. The conditions must **not** include:

■ Any clauses excluding responsibility for misrepresentation.
■ Any clauses saying they take no responsibility for staff or agents who make misleading statements.
■ Any clauses saying the firm is not liable for negligence by their staff in arranging your holiday.

The circumstances and conditions in which the holidaymaker may be liable to pay surcharges on the holiday should be set out clearly.

Quite apart from the ABTA code, tour operators and travel agents, whether or not they are members of the trade organization, are governed by the Unfair Contract Terms Act. In practice this means that booking conditions excluding liability for breaking the contract with you, for loss or damage caused by negligence or from giving a service which turns out to be different from that which the customer was led to expect have to be proved reasonable by the tour operator if the firm tries to rely on them. Probably such terms will be ineffective.

Insurance

This should be considered very carefully at the time of booking. Most tour operators offer insurance in their brochures, but before automatically saying 'yes', look very carefully at the terms they offer.

Checklist for Insurance

■ Compare the scheme in the brochure with insurance arranged independently.

■ Some firms insist on your taking out insurance through them and, if you want to arrange your own, they'll charge for theirs anyway. Ask.

■ Does it cover in full: medical expenses for pregnant women, people of any age and those already suffering from a disease or disability? Not all policies do.

■ Does it provide some cash on the spot if your money is stolen?

■ Is the medical cover sufficient? In America one requires a minimum of £50,000.

■ Always compare how much money is covered for loss, how much for luggage loss and so on, because the amount varies from one company to another.

Insurance claims

If you take out insurance through the tour operator – and most people do – then detach the page giving details of the insurance cover from the brochure and take it with you on holiday. This is important because it usually gives details of certain circumstances (such as losing money) where you must get a report of the theft from the local police to submit with any claim you make to the company.

If you do have a claim to make on your return from holiday, this should be made just as soon as possible on a special form, which you obtain from the insurance company. Normally you will have to include any receipted accounts you have for medical attention abroad and any other relevant documents, such as police reports.

If your claim is in connection with cancellation of the holiday, the cancellation certificate you get from the travel firm will be required.

At the time of booking ask about **fire safety** in your hotel. Fire regulations in some continental countries are not so strict as in the UK and there have been appalling hotel fires over the years.

Surcharges

These should be very clearly explained at the time of booking. The kind of charges likely to be made and why they are necessary must be spelled out.

■ **BEWARE** of special offers in brochures which make claims like 'no surcharges payable' and then have in very small print afterwards a phrase such as 'providing you book your holiday by 21 January'. Under the ABTA code there are certain points to which firms should adhere:

■ You must not be asked to pay currency surcharges less than 30 days before you go on holiday.

■ Other surcharges can be made nearer the departure date if they are as a result of cost increases over which the tour operator has no control, e.g. the cost of aviation fuel.

Alteration or Cancellation

The rules say that, if the holiday has to be altered, you must be told about it 'without delay', but they do not, unfortunately, specify exactly when. However, if some significant alteration is made the ABTA codes say that you must be offered a choice of a similar standard, or a total refund.

Cancellation of a holiday by the travel firm cannot happen after the date when you're due to pay the balance of the cost. There is one qualification, that is if the cancellation is due to hostilities, political unrest or if the holidaymaker simply refuses to pay the balance of the money he owes. If a trip is cancelled for such reasons then a speedy refund of your money should be forthcoming with another holiday of comparable standard as an alternative. However, a firm can cancel your holiday for any reason **before** the date the balance is due to be paid and in that case they must again offer either a refund or a holiday of similar standard.

On the other hand, if the customer cancels the holiday, the position is rather different. The rules vary from one tour operator to another but generally the penalty you incur is related to the length of time before departure date that you cancel.

Delays

Delays caused by such things as weather or strikes are largely a matter of insurance and should come under the terms of the policy you will have taken out through the tour operator. However, in addition to normal holiday insurance, many of the tour operators offer their own delay protection plans which are free of charge.

Overbooking

When you turn up at your foreign hotel, hot, dusty, just longing for a cup of tea and a nap only to discover that your room has already been assigned to someone else – that's overbooking! If overbooking isn't discovered till you are actually in the hotel then the company's local representative must find you alternative accommodation of the same standard. If you can only be squeezed into an attic room in the slummy end of town (officially described as 'location or facilities being inferior') then you must be offered some 'disturbance' compensation as well. Unfortunately, there is no set amount one can claim in these circumstances.

If the overbooking is discovered before the holidaymaker actually sets out, then the tour operator or travel agent must offer their client the choice of alternative accommodation of a similar standard or a full refund.

When Things Go Wrong

■ Make a complaint on the spot to the tour operator's rep at the local office. Contact their Head Office, if necessary.

■ If things can't be resolved at a local level, then wait until you get back home and go to your travel agent. To properly present your case it's important that you have noted down all the relevant details including dates and times and any action you took locally. In the case of a complaint abroad, it's not a bad idea to take along a small cassette recorder when you talk to the rep – this can be used later for reference if the dispute is taken to the travel agent.

■ If you can't get any result from personal discussion, then write a letter to the travel agent's Head Office giving details of your complaint and enclosing copies of any relevant correspondence.

■ No joy with the individual firm – then move on to its trade asociation, ABTA, which has a conciliation service. This service is free of charge and details with copies of correspondence should be sent to the Association of British Travel Agents, see Chapter Two. Alternatively you may contact your local CAB or Trading Standards Department.

■ If you are still struggling, make use of ABTA's independent arbitration scheme, which is run by the Chartered Institute of Arbitrators. Members must go to arbitration if you want to use this method. It usually works on a 'documents only' basis to keep costs down, so you don't have to go along to a hearing.

■ The alternative to arbitration is that the customer can pursue the case in the courts.

Holidaymakers who Live in Scotland or Northern Ireland

You should consider taking court action very carefully. This is quite simply because it might involve you in considerable long distance travel! If you read the small print in the booking conditions of many tour operators (including some of the largest) you will find that those living outside England would have to engage an English solicitor to handle the case for them. And that would involve difficulties of distance and expense.

Time-sharing

This is the latest way of buying holiday accommodation. What you buy, in effect, is the right to occupy a holiday home or flat for a particular period every year, usually falling on the same dates. Your right to occupation may be a 'lease' for a number of years or it may be for ever. The property management and maintenance are taken care of (although you pay for it) and you can do what you like with your week or two weeks – you can sell them, let them to someone else or lend them to a friend. But before you take to time-sharing, it's as well to bear in mind that precisely because it is a newish thing, there is no precise legislation to cover it.

Protection

The Timeshare Developers Association (TDA) (address in Chapter Two) is an association of major timeshare developers and the two major international timeshare exchange organizations. Members' contracts have a cooling off period of a minimum of five days during which buyers can cancel. Should there be a query of the actions of a TDA member, the association offers a conciliation service and an independent optional arbitration scheme conducted by the Chartered Institute of Arbitrators.